Acclaim for *Brain*

"In her outstanding book, Dora Camp chronicles the ordeal of helping her husband, Norm, rehabilitate from a near-fatal brain injury. Not content to be a sit-at-home wife, Dora turned this tragedy into a triumph of new life and meaning for her husband, for herself, and for the countless individuals and families she has touched through her selfless service and her support group, 'Brainstormers.' As a speech-language pathologist in the ABI support group at Pasadena City College, I have been privileged to know and work with both Norm and Dora. This is a must-read book, not just for those whose lives have been touched by brain injury, but for everyone."

— Rosemary Scott, MA-CCC

"Dora has a visceral understanding of loss without death. She has paved the way for thousands who live with brain-injured persons to find their way — while serving as a role model for preservation of the marriage vow "In sickness and in health."

— Rev. Alice Parsons Zulli, CGC,
CT Clinical Thanatologist

"Very inspirational, and a great resource for the families of those with traumatic brain injury. This is information you don't find in books written by professionals who treat TBI. I have spent many years treating this population, and this book gave me new insight into what family members go through while their loved ones are recovering from traumatic brain injury."

— Jan Adduci, Manager, Glendale
Adventist Medical Center,
Rehabilitative Medical Services

"Dora didn't limit herself to being a caregiver; she chose to be a source of help for other brain-injured people and their families. She formed a group called Brainstormers, which provides a safe place for dealing with the difficult emotions felt by both the spouse and the brain-injured person. With courage, humor, and love, she gives us practical tools for coping with the realities of caregiving, thus enabling us to accept and heal and have meaningful, joyful lives, despite our life-altering ordeals."

— Nancy Seal, Caregiver

BRAINSTORMING:

Life After Acquired Brain Injury

Dora Camp

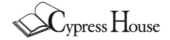
Cypress House

Cypress House
155 Cypress Street
Fort Bragg, CA 95437
(800) 773-7782
www.cypresshouse.com

Book design by Cypress House
Cover design by Elizabeth Petersen
Cover Illustration: Brand X Pictures

Library of Congress Cataloging-in-Publication Data

Camp, Dora.
    Brainstorming life after acquired brain injury / Dora Camp.-- 1st ed.
        p. cm.
    ISBN 1-879384-63-9 (pbk. : alk. paper)
    1. Camp, Norman--Health. 2. Brain damage--Patients--United States--Biography. 3. Brain damage--Patients--Rehabilitation. I. Title.

    RC387.5.C356 2005
    617.4'81044'092--dc22   2005002092

Printed in the United States

2   4   6   8   9   7   5   3   1

Dedicated to continuing education about brain injury. We must work to provide ample support systems for brain-injured individuals and their caregivers. The number of brain-injury survivors continues to grow, and they have the right to become the best that they can be.

Foreword

I am a neurologist, a Christian, and a survivor of the same injury Norm suffered: Hypoxic/Ischemic/Anoxic Encephalopathy. We are, in a way, modern-day Lazaruses. He and I, and Dora and Dot, our wives, *know* personally what this means. Theirs is a story of success, love, tragedy, more love, hope, and rebirth of the human spirit. Dora is the earthly embodiment of the Good Samaritan. Norm and others have "fallen by the side of the road." Dora has not "walked by," but has had compassion for them; she has "stopped to help." She has provided in abundance what all of us, the brain-soul-injured sufferers need: helping hands; a smiling face; joy; encouragement; and respect. As Harold Kushner wrote in *When Bad Things Happen to Good People,* Dora is *the act of God,* rushing to help in any way she can.

The world is blessed by her. We all must follow her example.

Glen Harper, M.D.

Acknowledgments

First, my thanks to Andrea Cagan, who was the "Wind Beneath My Wings." She is a gifted, caring, patient person without whom I could not have written this book.

Our son, Frank, who stands beside us, giving us a reason to keep trying.

To all my fellow Brainstormers, thank you for touching my life and teaching me how to be a strong, determined, persistent warrior for brain-injury education.

Finally, to my husband, Norm, who shows such great determination and strength, and uses his wonderful sense of humor to become the best he can be.

Contents

Chapter One

The Meeting

The Invitation

T he alarm clock rang at 4:30 A.M. I groaned, turned it off, and pushed myself out of bed. Stumbling into the bathroom, I splashed cold water on my face, marveling at being up at such an ungodly hour. The coyotes weren't even awake yet, I mused, peering into the darkness of the San Gabriel Mountains.

I loved living on the city's outskirts. True, it took a bit longer to get to meetings and to my office in downtown Los Angeles, where I worked for Pacific Bell. The office was on the seventeenth floor of a high-rise building next to the Harbor Freeway; it was worth the daily drive through heavy traffic to live among trees, raccoons, deer, lizards, mountain lions, and the coyotes' distant wailing. Los Angeles was a big change after having lived in northern California since 1948. I'd begun working for Pac Bell in 1961. But after my divorce, when my son and good friend, Frank, was grown, I decided to transfer and take a job in Southern California as a liaison with the California Public Utilities Commission. I ended up as a Xerox Account Manager, supervising an account team of five employees in LA and one in San Jose, a position that required a good bit of traveling.

Generally, I liked traveling. It brought enjoyable variation into my life; but being awake this early was pushing it. Still, I was looking forward to a week in San Diego, overseeing a large telephone installation in the Scripps Ranch area. I heard the thick tires of the Super Shuttle pull up in the driveway. The doorbell rang. I took a last look at the suitcase I'd packed last night, locked up the house, and said a silent prayer that all would be fine while I was gone. Then I settled into the shuttle and sped off to Burbank Airport.

After an exceptionally smooth flight, we landed in San Diego under a brilliant sunrise, the kind of perfect day for which the area is famous. After the usual stop to rent a compact car, I drove to the hotel where I'd be staying for the next week. Each day, I dressed in my "business best," met with my customers, and did everything I could to meet their requirements and make them happy. By late Friday, after a long week of perfecting the design of their new telecommunications system, I felt secure that the installation would go without a hitch.

I awoke early the next morning, put on a light cotton shorts set, tied the straps of my sandals, packed up the car, and headed for Xerox to make sure everything was working to the customer's satisfaction. Everyone seemed happy, so I headed to the San Diego Airport, feeling satisfied with the work I'd done. I liked working hard, but it wasn't so good for my nonexistent social life. It was easy to overlook having a good time, which was constantly eclipsed by my dedication to work. I really needed to do something about it. After all, I was forty-five, and wasn't getting any younger. *Later,* I thought, as I pulled into the airport entrance, stuck in a long line of people waiting to turn in their cars.

Feeling a bit rushed, I hurried to the check-in line. It wasn't surprising to discover that the small commuter plane had been delayed. After all, it was Saturday, not a popular day for passengers flying back to LA. I headed to the cocktail lounge, took advantage of the unusual quiet by spreading my paperwork over a couple of tables, and began to work on a new telecommunications design. I was lost in work when I heard the announcement that my flight was about to board. I gathered my things and headed outside the terminal. It was really hot out there, and sweat beads trailed down the inside of my blouse. I was anxious to get home after being away for a week. I missed my garden, and hoped it had survived the record hot temperatures during my absence.

"Is this the plane to Burbank?" I heard a man asking.

"I don't know," I said curtly. I'd occasionally met some weirdoes in the airport, and didn't want to be bothered by a stranger.

He read my body language and withdrew somewhat, but I was impressed with this man's demeanor as he sat beside me on the outdoor bench. It was something about his posture, and the way he wore his casual clothing, his straw hat, and loafers. He introduced himself as Norm. With his East Coast accent and a very impressive vocabulary, I found him quite attractive.

Still, I was hesitant to get to know him better. I had a good job, a great group of close friends, a beautiful house, an orange Corvette, and a Honda. I didn't want to rock the boat, since it seemed like every time I got romantically involved, it was too much work without satisfying results. I'd married when I was sixteen years old, and had a son, Frank, at eighteen, but the marriage broke up when Frank was one and a half. After raising a son by myself, I wasn't so anxious to jump back in. I'd become extremely independent over the years, and most of the men I'd met had been intent on changing me. I liked me just fine, and showing a lack of interest in changing for someone else usually ended the relationship. I'd dated over the years, had found the various men's personalities interesting, and had enjoyed the events I'd attended with each of them. Still, I hadn't yet found the person I wanted as a constant companion, someone to share my life with, but at the same time, I knew it might never happen, and that was fine.

As our line of five passengers started moving toward the plane, Norm got up and stood in front of me. I'm not so fond of flying in small commuter planes, but there were few choices from San Diego to Burbank. I rested my heavy briefcase on the ground beside me each time the line paused, fantasizing being home where I was about to start a well-earned two-week vacation. With no trips or activities planned, I anticipated days of planting the garden, catching up on some movies, and visiting with friends — and no alarm clocks!

As the line inched forward, I reached down for my briefcase; it was gone. I gasped, then noticed that my newest acquaintance, Norm, still in front of me, was carrying my burden.

"Excuse me," I said, "what are you doing with my briefcase?"

"I saw that it was heavy and I thought I'd carry it on board for you."

I would later learn that he wanted to make sure I sat beside him, but at the time, I was just glad he was helping me. When we were finally sitting side by side on the plane, Norm removed his shoes. "You look so comfortable with open-toed shoes and no socks," he said, "I wanted to copy you."

I was a little on guard. He seemed overly friendly and attentive. When the plane hit turbulence and he offered to hold my hand, I declined his invitation, but was impressed at what a gentleman he was. That was what got me talking, telling Norm about my job and my home in La Crescenta.

Norm said that he lived on the East Coast and worked at the Pentagon. I soon discovered that this well-educated gentleman with a great sense of humor was merely making interesting conversation, not pushing himself on me, and I began to relax. Before we landed, he asked if I liked to play tennis, since he was planning a game that same afternoon. To my own amazement, I agreed to join him, and gave him my telephone number, though I hadn't played since my grown son had been in grammar school. The tennis court seemed like a safe environment for getting to know someone.

When the flight attendant announced that it was 101 degrees in Burbank, it was obvious we needed to change plans. Norm had mentioned being a Redskins fan, and that they were playing that afternoon. I was surprised at how disappointed I felt, inwardly acknowledging that I wanted to get to know this man better. The next thing I knew, I'd invited him to my home to watch the game. It seemed safe enough, since my son, Frank, and his family had been staying there while I was in San Diego. If Norm were not the same gentleman he was at the airport and on the plane, I was safe with Frank there. For some reason, though, I trusted Norm, and my instincts were generally on target.

Watching the Game

I sat on the Super Shuttle heading for home, wondering what the hell I'd just done, inviting a man I hardly knew to my home. I was instantly distracted, though, thinking about how much there was to do before Norm arrived: piles of mail to open, a ton of bills to pay, and I'd need to fill the refrigerator.

The driver unloaded my luggage in front of my house. Dried-up pine needles and cones that had fallen from the trees crunched beneath my feet in the atrium. I opened the front door and smiled at finding Frank's clothes all over the living room. That was normal. Out on the deck, Frank, his wife, Kathy, and their son were in the hot tub enjoying the beautiful view of the Los Angeles basin. I threw them a kiss, hugged my wet grandson, mysteriously told them I was expecting company, and went off to do chores. I laughed, imagining Frank's reaction when Norm arrived. I'd divorced Frank's father when Frank was eighteen months old, and it had been just the two of us while my son was growing up. He was the man of the house, and intensely protective of his mother, which meant he usually didn't like the men I dated.

Oh well, it's my life, I thought, as I rushed around, cleaning, straightening, and hiding piles of stuff in the closet — until the doorbell rang. There had been no time to get groceries, so we'd have to make do with what was on hand. I opened the door to find Norm in a pair of shorts and his Redskins tee shirt. I introduced him to Frank and Kathy, and, after they excused themselves, Norm and I sat down to watch the game. The afternoon was easy and casual, as we shared a few drinks and cheered on his team. During the breaks, I learned that Norm loved his job as an oceanographer. It was quite a stroke of luck that he was scheduled to be in Los Angeles for the same two weeks that I was on vacation.

I marveled at the varied and accomplished life Norm had lived so far. He was a navy man, through and through. After graduating from Rhode Island College, he'd completed Officer Candidate School in Newport, Rhode Island, in 1965. His first assignment was aboard the USS *Bucannon* DDG 14 out of San Diego, where he spent two years in the engineering department as the Main Propulsion Assistant in charge of all boiler and engine rooms. Norm loved going to sea, enjoyed his fellow sailors, and spent half his time at sea, until attending Destroyer School back in Rhode Island. Up the military ladder he'd climbed; he was promoted to lieutenant and eventually became officer in charge of a ten-boat, fifty-sailor riverboat squadron in Vietnam.

Norm received two Bronze Star medals for heroic achievement in action. He was promoted to lieutenant commander and served as commanding officer of the USS *Opportune,* ARS 41, out of Little Creek, Virginia. His ship was evaluated as the best-performing ship in his squadron two years in a row. He eventually earned his Ph.D. in Oceanography from the Naval Postgraduate School in Monterey, California. Later he did a stint in Naples, Italy, where he was promoted to Commander, Department of the Navy. He also worked at the Pentagon as a commander. After twenty years in the navy, Norm retired from active duty in 1983, and was once again a civil servant, GS-15, working on research and development at the Pentagon.

He told me vivid stories of his world travels, of the countries where he'd lived, and where he'd skied the toughest slopes. I told him I'd never skied and hadn't traveled much, but was interested in doing both someday. Norm talked happily about golf, tennis, skiing, travel and the theater, making me laugh constantly. When he left, promising to call the next day, I didn't remember if the Redskins had won or lost, but I knew how much I was attracted to Norm.

I wandered back into the living room where we'd just spent our first hours together. I picked up the empty glasses, wondering whether Norm was feeling the same emotions I felt. I couldn't have been more surprised to have met someone, on the plane, no less, who was so much fun to be with. He seemed to enjoy my independent personality, and he was playful, communicative, and very smart. I'd enjoyed the visit; apparently, so had he, and now I was left with a very important question: Will he call me tomorrow?

Falling In Love

I was delighted when Norm called the next day with an invitation to see the Los Angeles production of "CATS." I love the theater, and frenziedly wondered what to wear, feeling like a teenager again. Wanting to impress him, I chose my favorite blue suit, and when he rang the doorbell at seven sharp, I was totally excited. But why was he wearing sunglasses at night? "Leave it to me," he said, laughing at himself, "to forget my glasses." Those prescription sunglasses were all he had, but it didn't seem to bother him. I smiled. Wasn't that just like an intellectual of Norm's caliber, to be the absentminded professor!

We loved the play, and when we went out dancing afterward, I met several of Norm's friends, whom I thought were terrific. We saw "CATS" twice during those two romantic weeks, because we both enjoyed it so much.

Meeting Norm at the beach for dinner after work one day, I found him devastated by the unexpected death of a close friend. The man had committed suicide, and Norm was having a hard time coming to grips with his untimely death. I was glad to be able to comfort him in my own small way. By the time my two vacation weeks were up, I'd gotten to know Norm and liked who he was. We were both forty-five, and had become such strong, independent people that I'd initially feared we wouldn't be compatible, but it seemed to work in reverse. Our similar penchants for taking a leadership role for most of our lives created a mutual understanding and harmony between us that I never could have predicted.

When it was time for Norm to return to DC, I knew I'd miss him, but was also glad he was leaving. My feelings for a man who lived 3000 miles away were becoming too strong. Saying goodbye was hard; we both knew we'd see one another again, but we also knew that our next meeting depended on his next business meeting, as yet unscheduled.

During the next months, Norm and I ran up a couple of huge phone bills. We just couldn't stand to be apart, and it seemed that with each phone call our relationship grew stronger, until I knew I was in love for the first time. I had found my Mr. Wonderful at this late stage in life, and I wasn't about to give him up. Unwilling to wait any longer, I flew to Washington to see Norm in October. I was overjoyed when he met me at the airport, even though he laughed at my lightweight clothing. I was a California girl who'd never been on the East Coast in winter, and I had no idea how cold it could get.

As a newcomer in Washington, I was excited to tour the historic city with a real insider. I climbed into Norm's gray, 4-door Volvo sedan. *What a contrast,* I thought, as we drove along the countryside, heading toward Maine in October — *Norm with his conservative sedan, and me with my orange Corvette.* I actually belonged to two Corvette clubs, which says a great deal about the difference in our personalities, yet we liked doing the same things.

The weather was cooling, the tourists had gone home, and the leaves were turning colors in the crisp autumn air. We slept in bed & breakfast inns all along the way, making no reservations or schedules; we stayed where we pleased. One night we got a drink in a bar where the New England accents were so thick that I wondered if they were speaking English. Norm continually wore me out with his insatiable excitement, like the time he woke me up at 2 A.M. so we could see the sunrise on Mt. Cadillac in the freezing cold. When we arrived at the top of the mountain, there were people with tripods, colored lenses, and large cameras. I marveled at how much they had to love photography to be there so early and endure the freezing temperatures.

Then there was the day in Bar Harbor when I was so tired that I slept in the car while Norm went shopping. He woke me after he'd rushed back to the car, got in, and said, "I just bought you an 'engaged to be engaged' rock."

Slightly bleary-eyed, I put on the ring, which was indeed a big rock — one of those adjustable kinds you might find in a Cracker Jack box. He talked me into accompanying him to the store where he bought it, to tell the salesladies that I'd accepted the "pre-engagement" ring. They were thrilled. I continued shopping with Norm. Like two kids in a candy store, between new clothing, pictures, and brass figurines, we had a hard time fitting all our purchases into the car. On our way home, we stopped at a lobster restaurant, where we told the owner we had just gotten pre-engaged. He told us some stories in a cute New England accent, which I was starting to understand, and sent us off with an engagement gift: a cooler packed with two live Maine lobsters that we could cook when we got to Norm's condo.

When I got on the plane to go back home, I knew I had fallen in love. I felt empty without Norm. He added a great deal to my life, and I wanted to spend lots more time with him, but we lived 3000 miles apart and both had successful jobs we weren't willing to give up. We courted for the next two years, meeting in various towns during our business travels, extending our time away so we could take mini-vacations together. I wanted to be with Norm, he wanted to be with me, and we would figure out a way. But the icing on the cake was that Frank, a big guy at six feet three inches and 250 pounds, who usually tried to intimidate my boyfriends, adopted Norm from the start, and we all looked forward to being friends for life. To this day, the two men in my life are great companions, and I always like to recall the day that "Frank adopted Norm," not the other way around.

Chapter Two

Nesting

Early Retirement

As I sped across the country to Washington for Norm's retirement party, I gazed out the window of the plane as we sailed over a soft blanket of cloud cover. The flight was smooth, but my brain was in enough turbulence to make it seem choppy.

Norm's first retirement had occurred before I met him, on October 1, 1983. He'd been forty-three when he left active service and became a civil servant at the Pentagon. Now, in June 1987, I was about to attend his second retirement celebration. At the same time, after two years of long-distance courtship, we were making our relationship permanent by moving in together. It was Norm's idea, and his voice had sounded completely steady when he announced he was quitting his job and moving to the West Coast. This decision was not sudden, he explained excitedly. He had thought it out, the time was right, and if he waited and got involved in a new government project, it might be four or five more years before we could really be together.

I'd felt perfectly safe during our courtship, knowing I could always return to my solitude. I loved Norm, but the thought of living together seemed so real and scary. How would it feel to live with a man now that we were both in our mid-forties? Did we know each other well enough? Would our relationship continue to blossom? Why didn't I feel as sure as Norm sounded?

He was always so clear in his decisions, no second-guessing or regrets. *I could learn a thing or two about decision making from Norm,* I thought, recalling his enthusiasm about our moving in together. His excitement was so contagious that it excited everyone around him when he talked, with deliberation and clarity, about his latest decision. How could I ever have guessed that I would someday be making *all* the decisions for both Norm and me?

The logistics of the move, as opposed to my emotional state, were simple. Norm was content to handle things by himself, which took all the pressure off of me. Maybe it wouldn't be so scary after all. When I really thought about it, I was tired of our long-distance relationship, and was ready to start a new life with Norm, my best friend. So why were my hands trembling? But when Norm met me at the airport and wrapped his arms around me, all my fears disappeared. One step at a time, I told myself, as I prepared to celebrate Norm's retirement.

Nick, Norm's boss, held the party at his own home. A retired rear admiral, Nick had earned a Ph.D. from MIT and later became director of the Woods Hole Oceanographic Institute. He was also a Navy SEAL. A world traveler, he often visited foreign countries and became a part of their research teams. His huge, elegant house reflected a life well lived by a man whose motto was, "Retire and go extreme." The last I heard, he was living in Fairbanks, working as vice president of the University of Alaska. He is a risk taker, a hard worker, and a lover of life.

Dressed casually, Nick greeted us at the front door. Looking into his eyes, I saw immediately that he was the kind of guy who tolerated no bullshit, and I really liked that. He invited us into the living room, where all of Norm's coworkers were gathered to honor his career. I couldn't have been more proud of him, but as the night progressed, I noticed that Nick was slowly shedding his clothing, starting with his shoes and socks. Maybe he just liked being comfortable. After all, this was his house. But when he removed his shirt, I asked Norm what was going on.

"He's a Navy SEAL," Norm told me with a big smile, "and he isn't afraid to be himself." I only hoped that "being himself" didn't include stripping down to the buff and running around. But then if his wife, Patty, didn't mind, why should I?

Patty had prepared heaping platters of salads, meats, fruits, dips, and desserts. As we ate, and drank toasts to Norm, I met some of his wonderful coworkers. I have since become friends with a number of them, especially Nick and Patty, whom we've visited in Virginia. In fact, when Norm suffered his accident and was forced to start his life over again, Nick, who had a lifelong interest in the workings of the brain, lent me several books on brain function. "If you don't understand the brain," he said, "you'll never be able to manage people."

Toward the end of the retirement party, Nick presented Norm with a door that had been sawed in two, featuring a big hole in the bottom half. Nick told the party that Norm had tried to enter through that door at work one morning, but couldn't get it open. He'd kicked it, and his foot had gone through to the other side. Nick had removed it, sawed it in half, and was presenting it to Norm as a remembrance. It was a wonderful thought, and got a great laugh, but what do you do with a door with a big hole in it? To this day it sits under the workbench in our garage, one of those things you can't do anything with, but you just can't let it go.

When we left the party late that night, heading for Norm's home in Virginia, I had a warm feeling, and remembered my friend's advice about relationships: "If you really want to learn about a person, get to know their friends." I liked Norm's friends, I adored Norm, and I felt secure that we were doing the right thing.

I returned to California the following night, while Norm stayed in DC to pack up his furniture and have it shipped out West. I was wondering where I would put the extra pieces, shoring myself up to face the new stuff that was about to enter my home, but Norm had a surprise for me. He was taking me to Maui before we started our cohabitation. I couldn't have been more excited. Those kinds of spontaneous decisions, like suddenly going to Hawaii or having an equally exciting adventure somewhere else, might be what I miss the most since Norm's injury. At the time, he even talked me into allowing a friend to receive his furniture at my place in La Crescenta. Left to my own devices, I'd have postponed the trip until his things arrived, but Norm constantly showed me how to take more chances and enjoy life to the fullest.

It turned out that our trip to Maui couldn't have been timed better. The hibiscus and bougainvillea were in full bloom, trailing the sides of the highway, and the topaz ocean was so warm that we could swim and snorkel all day long among the sparkling coral reefs and brightly colored tropical fish. *One week wasn't long enough,* I kept repeating to myself when we got back home to face a load of furniture that had to be added to my home. But the trip had left me feeling renewed, raring to go, and deeply in love with Norm.

Putting our lives together was the next step, and we were both committed to life being better than before.

Combining Lives

I couldn't begin to imagine how the new furniture would fit. I take pride in decorating houses and had no need for additional furniture, but Norm helped me approach the situation lightly, knowing that it would all work out. And it did — after some rearranging and blending. An extra couch here, a table there, and we were officially living together.

Norm wasn't the type to sit around, though, even in retirement. After a number of interviews, he took a position in the corporate world as vice president of a research and development organization in Van Nuys, California. While Norm settled into his new job and I continued with my own, eating out became one of our favorite pastimes, since neither of us had a good relationship with the kitchen.

It hadn't always been that way, at least for me. I cooked all the time when I was raising my son, but I'd done enough cooking for one lifetime, I felt, so Norm and I frequented our favorite restaurants, where he appreciated all the different tastes and textures. After his injury, when he forgot what food was for, and which foods were good for him, I got reintroduced to my kitchen, preparing the kinds of meals that would nourish Norm and keep us both trim.

Our Home Away From Home

When Norm sold his house in Virginia soon after moving in with me, he had eighteen months to reinvest his capital gains from the sale. He was interested in buying something in a resort area, but wasn't familiar with California. Considering Norm's love of skiing, I suggested we take a look at real estate in the Big Bear Lake area, a two-hour drive from La Crescenta. I'd been there many times with the other members of my Corvette club, staying in rustic cabins and enjoying the tranquil small-town atmosphere. Why not own a home there, where Norm could ski and I could enjoy the peacefulness of the lake? Determined to find what we were looking for, we took a trip up there, checked into a motel, and found ourselves a real estate agent.

The night before we found our new place, we were awakened at 3 A.M. by some noisy neighbors in the motel, shuffling their skis around, anticipating their day on the slopes. Unable to get back to sleep, we decided to explore the resort town in the middle of the night. We were delighted to find that Big Bear Boulevard, even partially covered with snow, had a tiny donut shop that stayed open all night. When we walked in, the smell of fresh bread and donuts made us feel ravenous, and we ordered fresh maple bars and coffee. The baker didn't look pleased to see anyone so early in the morning. In fact, he seemed to resent the intrusion, but we didn't care. We devoured the hot coffee and pastries as if we hadn't eaten in a week, smiling contentedly as we headed back to our room to catch a few hours' sleep before our appointment with the real estate agent. I dozed off, dreaming of the perfect cabin for our home away from home.

Bob, the Realtor, helped us into his SUV and drove us around Big Bear's Moonridge area, with spectacular views of both the Goldmine and Snow Summit ski resorts. We looked at a few places that weren't quite right, but when we pulled up to a large cabin under construction, a FOR SALE sign in the window, I was enchanted. We crossed two boards set up to create a bridge, entered the unfinished cabin, and saw that it needed work on the floors, walls, rails, stairs, and many other places. But wouldn't that give us an opportunity to make personal decisions on the unfinished items, designing them in our own way? I loved the gray rock fireplace, its mantle made from a large tree stump and finished with gleaming varnish. Two bay windows looked out on the slopes, and I could imagine sitting there with a cup of tea and a good book, watching the skiers sailing down the mountain.

The kitchen was small, with off-white appliances and a variety of leaf-patterned tiles scattered among the plain beige ones. The oak cabinets matched the wooden kitchen floor, a large neon light-box fixture covered almost the entire ceiling, and I could see that a small table and chairs would fit nicely beside the stove. It was perfect, so Norm wrote down the number of the builder from the sign out front, and we called to get the particulars. When we learned that this was the builder's first house, that he took enormous pride in it, and would be happy to complete it to our specifications, we made an offer. A few hours later, the place was ours!

The builder happily agreed to our requested changes, like tiling the front entry as well as upgrading railings, carpets, and wood floors. As we stashed Norm's skis, poles, and boots in the special closet the builder made for us, we were thrilled that this would be our mountain retreat for years to come. I'll never forget the delivery team from Sears who carried the brand-new washer and dryer down twenty-five steep inside stairs into the laundry room.

All we had left to do was move some of Norm's furniture out of the La Crescenta house and into the Big Bear House, which made the old house roomier and the new one cozier. After we purchased brass beds, dressers, side tables and lamps for both bedrooms, we had officially finally moved in. We fell asleep on the couch that first night, gazing at the slopes of Goldmine, fantasizing being out there in the morning, enjoying the pristine white world of snow.

Wedding Bells

It wasn't long before our vacation home was filled with our dearest friends and family, and not only in the winter. During the summer months, we would make a lunch and head to a perfect place to water-ski — a cove adjacent to the lake, where fishing boats were prohibited. The cove had a safe space for takeoffs and landings, and we spent the day eating, swimming, water-skiing, and listening to music. On our way home, we often docked at The Tale of the Whale restaurant for refreshments and live music, a period of time I would give anything to relive. On weekends, the restaurant had two bands, one outside on the deck and the other inside, where you could be in the warmth and out of the sun at midday. The vocal groups got everyone involved in sing-alongs, and, small though the dance floor was, we kicked up our heels, dancing, singing, and laughing our nights away.

I wonder sometimes if I enjoyed it enough when it was happening, but you know what they say about hindsight. I can say for sure that Norm and I lived our lives to the fullest during those first two years, culminating in planning our marriage ceremony for Sept. 5, 1989. I was about to become Mrs. Norm Camp, and, as we thought about where we wanted to do the deed, I couldn't have been happier.

It didn't take long to decide, since we loved Hawaii so much. And it wasn't difficult to entice sixteen friends to join us in the Hawaiian Islands for our wedding. Every bit of it was an adventure, as Norm and I contacted Reverend Sterling, who came highly recommended, and we went to the local party store that doubled as a distributor of marriage licenses.

In most of the preparations, I was allowed to relax as Norm took over planning the travel and lodging arrangements for our various guests arriving from Texas, Florida, Washington, DC, and California. In fact he was so organized and did such a great job that everyone arrived in Hawaii within the same hour. That was Norm back then, an efficient, brilliant, fun-loving man with a take-control attitude. For our wedding dinner, we chose a restaurant beside a grouping of massive black lava rocks, where ocean waves splashed continuously against the shore.

One afternoon, I walked through an abundance of green banana trees and other tropical flowers and plants growing along the path leading from the condo to the Kona Surf Resort. There I found a small white chapel hidden among the foliage, completely surrounded by water. With its hardwood floors, bench seating, and colorful stained glass behind the rectory, the chapel reminded me of the churches I had seen on the East Coast. I fell in love with it, and to my delight, discovered that the Kona Surf Resort was willing to rent it out, music and all, for our September wedding.

I walked down the aisle in a soft beige lace dress, and Norm wore a white linen suit. The best man wore a pink floral Hawaiian shirt and white pants, while my maid of honor wore light-colored linen. We all had brightly colored aromatic leis around our necks. When Norm kissed me, I knew I was married for good, for better or worse, in sickness and in health and in brain injury — a huge and as yet unknown part of our future together.

The First Collapse

T hank God we didn't know our real future as we stayed in Maui for a week by ourselves, savoring our love and the relaxation and facing a brand new cycle in our lives. In 1990, Pac Bell offered me an early retirement package that I couldn't refuse. I relaxed into an easier life, and Norm, along with six other expert skiers from his workplace, took a "Men Only" ski trip once a year. So far they had ventured into Canada, Colorado, and Utah, using helicopter drops to take them far away from where less proficient skiers dared descend the mountains. These short vacations from Norm gave me the opportunity to invite my female friends for a week in Big Bear, where we were busy conquering the bunny slopes. That was another great part of Norm's and my relationship: we were secure enough to enjoy our time apart as well as our time together.

In February 1991, the men were headed to Colorado for their annual trip, and I was making plans for the women to gather in Big Bear. Norm called once to ask me what I wanted from Colorado. He was always thinking of me, and I had a wonderful time with the girls as we celebrated my niece's fortieth birthday. Soon after I arrived home, I got a call from Norm, who was due home later that evening, telling me he had collapsed in the Denver airport.

I was stunned. There had been no indications whatsoever that Norm was ill, and I was terribly upset to learn that he had ended up in the emergency room of a local hospital. I asked question after question, trying to make sense of what had happened. Was he feeling sick when he collapsed? He'd just had a complete physical, was in good health, and had shown absolutely no symptoms of heart trouble, such as chest pains, discomfort in his arms, or shortness of breath.

Still, that collapse should have been the warning. It was the moment when a defibrillator should have been implanted in Norm's chest, but we were never told that was an option. I felt helpless, since Norm was in Denver and I was home, but he assured me that his friend, Lance, was by his side, and they would leave in the morning, just as soon as Norm was released from the hospital.

Needless to say, I didn't sleep much that night. I finally dropped off a few minutes before the phone rang. It was 5:30 A.M., and Norm was on his way to the airport to come home. They had found nothing wrong. When Norm pulled up in front of the house, I threw my arms around him and smothered him with kisses. He said he felt fine, and he looked fine, too, but I made him an appointment with his doctor, just to make sure.

On February 4, 1991, Norm was given a complete work-up, including urine, blood, and EKG and stress tests. All the results were negative for heart problems, but, as a precautionary measure, the doctor suggested that Norm wear a holtor monitor, a portable electrocardiogram that would record all his heart activity over a twenty-four-hour period. He strapped on the monitor, which can reveal abnormal heart rhythms, and I dropped him off at work.

The next day, with me acting as designated driver until we were sure Norm was all right, I drove him back to the doctor's office, where they removed the monitor and sent it to a lab for analysis. We had heard nothing by February 6, and Norm went to work as usual, but by mid-morning, the doctor called Norm's office. He had just gotten the results and insisted that Norm drop everything and go straight to Midland Medical Center with an overnight bag. As Norm and I each headed for the hospital from different directions, neither of us knew what was wrong, but we knew that it must be serious.

We soon found out that Norm was having episodes of what they called "supraventricular tachycardia," a fancy name for an arrhythmia that impairs the heart's ability to pump blood efficiently. He had also had over 410 episodes of something else called "ventricular tachycardia," which involves a rapid, uncoordinated rhythm that begins from an abnormal trigger in the ventricles. The two conditions combined can be fatal, possibly leading to cardiac arrest and total stoppage of circulation.

I was terrified when they hooked Norm up to an intravenous injection while he was still registering episodes. What did it mean? On February 7, Norm underwent cardiac catheterization so he could be evaluated for coronary disease. They found nothing. When he was wheeled back to his room, I watched him sit there motionless, doctor's orders, for six hours, a bag of sand directly over the incision making sure it remained closed so he wouldn't bleed to death. It was strange and disturbing to see Norm, my rock and my love, in such a vulnerable state.

I hoped to take him home the next day, but they weren't finished with him yet. They had scheduled him for an "electrophysiologic stimulation study," during which they hoped to find the origin of his heart problem. But the results of this test, too, were negative, allowing them to absolutely exclude coronary disease. They loaded Norm up with medications and he returned to work.

Perhaps his collapse was a part of it, but for a variety of reasons, Norm felt unhappy in his present job. I suppose he had realized while he was lying in the hospital as they tested his heart, that life was too short to work at something that wasn't fulfilling. So, when an East Coast research and development company offered Norm a position starting a new division on the West Coast, he jumped at the offer. Grant, a good friend and talented scientist, decided to join him; I found them an office in Calabasas, and fitted it out with furniture and equipment.

Business was slow at first, even after I was replaced with a real-live secretary, but a year and a half in, everything started to pick up. Norm hired extra scientists, found larger quarters in a high-rise in Woodland Hills, and the business flourished, as did our marriage. We made new friends, and were active in golfing, horseback riding, hiking, and, of course, skiing in Big Bear. As good as Norm was, he had signed up for classes to improve his balance and help him conquer the advanced moguls. After his first class, he came home with big bruises on both hips, but the smile on his face was all I needed to see to make me feel all right about it.

In the end, I was certain I had bucked the odds by meeting someone, falling in love, and getting married when we were both in our mid-forties. Now that the heart scare was over, I didn't care that love had come a little on the late side. It was there and would remain the one constant in our lives — even after Norm lost his capacity to speak the right words to express the depth of his love for me.

Chapter Three

A Life-changing Moment

T
he ominous drone of the siren didn't grab my attention; a common
sound in any city, it blended into the background noise. And just like
everyone else, I was sure it had nothing to do with me. Norm and his
close friend, Ricardo, were taking a bike ride, and were such experienced cy-
clists that I never had to worry about them, even when they braved packed
highways, whizzing cars missing them by inches.

I continued looking in at storefronts, killing time, while my friend, Rosie,
was busy preparing a birthday feast for the party she was throwing for her
husband, Ricardo, that night. Rosie was such a proficient cook, and so well
organized as she sliced, peeled, and cut up fruits and vegetables at record
speed, that she really didn't need my help. The best thing I could do was
keep out of her way, which was why I was window shopping on the main
drag in Del Mar, having agreed to be back at the house by 4 P.M. to help
with the decorations.

That morning, Norm and I had driven from La Crescenta to Del Mar,
a beach town adjacent to San Diego, to attend the party. Or rather, I had
driven, while Norm made phone calls (he didn't like driving and I didn't
mind it), wishing everyone a Happy New Year, since we'd be spending the
night in San Diego. It had seemed like any other day, but, thinking back, I
was surprised when Norm placed my address book on the dashboard, put
down the phone, and sighed. It wasn't odd that he was using my address
book because he'd misplaced his own. In fact, that was laughably normal in
Norm's case. But when he complained about feeling tired, wondering if it
was a mistake to go bike riding that afternoon, he got my attention. Norm
usually had an endless supply of energy, working and playing harder than

the rest of us, and then urging us all to keep going. But then there were the three packs of cigarettes a day that he couldn't seem to kick, as much as he hated addictions of any kind. Maybe his breathing was being affected.

I could only hope he'd stop smoking before he got sick, but I decided not to ruin our trip by nagging. After an easy drive, we checked into the Hyatt Islandia, and Norm changed into his cycling clothes. He was obviously feeling better, so I put away my concerns as we got back in the car and headed to Ricardo and Rosie's house.

Ricardo, a brilliant engineer who'd earned his Ph.D. from Cal Tech in Pasadena, had been appointed to head DARPA, an arm of the Defense Department, in DC. Norm and Ricardo had become business associates in 1979 when Norm, then working for the government, had managed Ricardo's Research and Development project out of Sherman Oaks, California. Norm flew there occasionally from Washington to oversee the work he and Ricardo did on several projects together before Norm retired.

The two had kept up their relationship, and their mutual respect had blossomed into a rich and rewarding friendship over the years. When Ricardo and Rosie sold their house in Sherman Oaks and moved to Del Mar, we continued seeing them socially. I really liked them both, and we all seemed to share a similar sense of humor. For example, Ricardo was an avid long-distance cyclist, and, as a joke for his birthday, Norm had bought his friend "the perfect gift."

"I know you're getting a little old to balance on your bike properly, so I have just the thing," Norm planned to say that night, as he held out a pair of training wheels for Ricardo's racing bike. The fact that Ricardo logged fifty miles a day on his bike several days a week would make it all the funnier, and we could hardly wait for the party and the presentation of the gift.

Rosie, Italian through and through, loved giving parties, for which she cooked up delectable feasts. Whenever we were there, I looked forward to her homemade sausages and pastas, golden cheese omelets cooked to perfection, or crispy bacon and eggs Benedict. After taking her daily long walk along the ocean, Rosie would return home with bakery goods and brew up some coffee, or we'd all walk to a nearby restaurant to have fresh fish or a salad.

Now, it was December 31, 1996. I smiled when I thought about Norm and Ricardo leaving the house on their bikes that afternoon. It was another gorgeous day in Del Mar, and the men were both dressed in tight-fitting bike pants and the bright-colored shirts that would alert people a long distance away that they were coming. I'd watched them click their bicycle shoe cleats into the special pedals, and then they were off.

Norm always looked sexy to me in his cycling gear, and that morning had been no exception. I was lucky to still be so in love with my husband, I thought, as I continued shopping, and to find him physically irresistible after seven years of marriage. I'd seen him and Ricardo earlier, huffing and puffing their way up a hill that went into the center of town. We had all waved as I sped past them in the car. *Boys and their toys,* I'd thought happily, as I found a space in a crowded parking garage.

I wandered into a shoe store and smiled. Just yesterday, I had stood at the door of Norm's closet in our home, gazing at a variety of single shoes strewn across the floor, abandoned by their mates, which were buried beneath piles of used clothing. I shook my head and closed the door. That was Norm's territory, a real no-man's land for anyone but him. As opposed to his one-pointed focus and the meticulous way he worked with his scientists on his oceanographic research projects, at home he was ever the absentminded professor, messy and disorganized, with little interest in the daily upkeep of our home. To this day, he doesn't see the connection between absentmindedness and extreme intelligence, but I've observed the same kind of behavior in some of Norm's brightest colleagues. Many of their wives would pack a lunch in a brown bag for their "brainy" husbands, because the men would otherwise forget to eat. Once, an acclaimed scientist showed up in Boston for a meeting that was being held in San Francisco. At least I wasn't the only wife with a forgetful husband.

Oh well, finding his shoes is his problem, I'd told myself, as I went about the household chores. I'd always been an organized person who resented wasting precious time looking for lost items, but if Norm wanted to go searching for his shoes every time he needed to go out, so be it. I knew better than to interfere with the way he functioned, which was one of the reasons our marriage had worked out so well. If Norm's behavior in any particular area didn't directly impact me, I left it alone, and if we disagreed about something, we usually agreed not to discuss it, unless it was crucial to our immediate well-being. With intensely strong personalities like ours, this was a perfect way to stop arguments before they arose and to avoid fighting battles in which neither of us would give in.

I'd walked around the house, straightening photographs, fluffing pillows, and picking up newspapers and magazines. The legendary seven-year itch was nowhere in sight, not even when I'd get a call from Norm at work, wondering how I let him leave the house wearing two different socks or, in extreme situations, a pair of shoes that didn't match. I'd laugh, so would he, and he'd return to his project, promptly forgetting about all things domestic as he buckled down to solve advanced problems in his current government research project.

Since Norm and I had married, life had changed in a wonderful way. Though retired from Pacific Bell, with a retirement package that was impossible to pass up, I was hardly ready to sit around the house, watching TV and eating bonbons. Having worked in the telecommunications field since my early twenties, I was aware of a void in the area of overcharges on telephone bills since deregulation had occurred. I set up a home office with desk, computer, fax machine, and printer and I was in business. While Norm traveled and I worked at home, I had time to flex my creative muscles as I decorated, painted, rearranged art and furniture, and made up beautiful floral arrangements. After decorating baseball caps with ribbons, beads, and stones, I started selling them to stores in La Jolla, but stopped when it became "a job," as I was no longer interested in rushing around to meet supply demands.

I just did my work and concentrated on creative endeavors that forced me to be innovative — yet another skill that would later be crucial to Norm's recovery when our lives were turned upside down. I simply enjoyed my time, indulging in luxuries like soaking in the tub and dying my hair while my husband was away on business. Although I loved being with Norm, his absences had helped me adjust to married life, offering me some free time when I didn't have to think about making dinner, doing laundry, or keeping track of social commitments that Norm promptly forgot as soon as he'd made them. All in all, it was a great time in my life; today I fantasize having *just one* of those days back, when nothing was required of me, a luxury I haven't experienced since the dreadful accident.

I even look back with nostalgia at the times when Norm called me from an airport parking lot in some seemingly godforsaken place to tell me he couldn't find the car. Norm traveled a couple of days each week for his work back then, placing him in airports all over the country. When I suggested that he park in the same spot or at least in the same vicinity in each airport, I little knew that I was beginning the tedious work of reorganizing Norm's habits. Later, when his brain could no longer hold vital information, the habit of parking in the same spot would become a critical survival strategy that he would use for the rest of his life. At the time, though, since my parking method got him from place to place faster, he simply incorporated the suggestion into his day-to-day life.

I see now that it was a stroke of good luck that both Norm and I liked being on the go, considering all the trips, vacations, meetings, and social events associated with his business. And then, Norm had made it perfectly clear that he was not interested in being the in-house handy man. I was fine with that, hiring someone else to do the odd jobs required to keep a home in good repair.

I continued moving through the different Del Mar boutiques, all quaintly decorated with soft colors and expensive clothing and furniture, everything enhanced with tasteful Christmas ornaments. The sirens sounded again as I bought three decorative plates. *There must have been quite an accident,* I thought as I checked my watch, noticing that it had begun to rain. It was 3:30 and I was more than ready to leave, since my feet were tired and I wanted to sit down and relax in a dry place. I headed back to the parking lot, found my car, and, despite the heavy traffic and the rain, pulled up outside Ricardo and Rosie's house at 4 P.M. sharp. I felt good about being on time, but when I looked at Rosie's face as she ran toward me along the front walkway, my entire body tightened.

The Accident

I could barely understand Rosie when she said breathlessly, "There's been an accident. Norm fell off his bike." Ricardo had called and asked Rosie to come to the highway so he could load his and Norm's bikes into her car. She had arrived at the accident location to find policemen and emergency vehicles, their lights flashing and sirens wailing. I grabbed my face with my hands. Oh, my God, those sirens had been for Norm! And I had continued shopping, a few hundred feet from where he lay, as if I hadn't a care in the world.

I jumped into Rosie's car without a word and we sped across Del Mar, heading to a nearby hospital in Encinitas. On the way, she told me what little she knew. Ricardo and Norm had stopped for a red light and Norm had lit a cigarette, commenting that he felt tired, but thought he could continue and take a nap at the hotel before the party. Then Ricardo had ridden on ahead of Norm, taking extra care on the slippery highway, since it had started to rain. When he looked back and didn't see his friend close behind him, Ricardo turned around to go find him, then jumped off his bike and ran the few feet to where Norm was lying on the ground; he had no idea what had happened to Norm, and wondered whether a car had hit him. It was impossible to believe that someone with Norm's cycling experience had fallen, unconscious, just like that.

Ricardo had seen a man with a cell phone standing beside Norm, reporting the accident to 911. They had dispatched an ambulance, fire trucks, and emergency response teams in record time, since they were already in the area, responding to a false alarm. I often wonder how long it would have taken them to get to Norm if that false alarm hadn't happened. It could easily have been too late, as Ricardo stood, devastated, aware that his friend, covered in blood, was dying and there was nothing he could do.

Skin was missing from the left side of Norm's face, blood oozed from his nose, and his legs and arms also had patches of skin missing, with large gashes that were spilling blood onto the pavement. Ricardo had tried to remove Norm's helmet to see if he had broken his neck, but the emergency team brushed him aside as they began resuscitation, all the while cutting off Norm's clothes and starting an intravenous line. Norm did not respond when they placed the external defibrillator on his chest. The first shock didn't revive his heart, nor did the second. Ricardo had watched Norm's face turning blue when the third shock from the paddles didn't cause him to register a heartbeat, either. But the fourth, thank God, produced results. After twenty minutes with this experienced team of paramedics, Norm was stabilized enough to be transported to Scripps Encinitas Hospital. Ricardo had ridden there in a police car, where he was waiting for us to arrive.

I listened to what Rosie was telling me, but could hardly make sense of it. All I could say was, "How much farther? How much longer? Are we there yet?" I needed to see Norm and find out how serious his injuries were.

When we pulled up to the emergency room entrance, I burst out of the car before Rosie had come to a full stop. I found Ricardo seated in the waiting room, looking shocked but composed. "He didn't have his ID with him, and they can't proceed until you tell them who he is."

I rushed to the reception desk. "I need to see my husband right now!" I said. But it seemed that providing them with Norm's insurance information took precedence over everything else — even his life! I rifled my wallet and came up with the insurance card that seemed so damned important, and then took a seat in the waiting area. They had no news for me as yet, but promised to keep me informed. I sat, desolate and frantic, fearful that Norm would be dead by the time I was allowed to see him. And I hadn't even said goodbye.

While waiting, Ricardo and I distracted ourselves by figuring out how to notify people that Norm was in trouble. I called Frank first, who was living in a small northern California town called Exeter. When he promised to be on the next plane, I called my stepdaughter, Lindy, who was skiing in Tahoe. She would be here as soon as possible, and my stepson, John, would leave DC in the next few days.

While I was figuring out who else to call, a nurse approached me. "Are you ready to see your husband?" she asked. We headed through the swinging doors with the No ADMITTANCE sign, then to a small waiting room with a table and two folding chairs. "Your husband is in serious condition," she said. I heard her next words through a fog. "I think you should call anyone who needs to see him, because he might not make it." But she couldn't tell me exactly what was wrong with him, because she didn't know.

I followed the woman in white down a long sterile hallway, stopping in front of what appeared to be an operating room. I stepped in, blinded by bright lights hanging from the ceiling, reflecting off the staff's green scrubs. Their white masks and hats made the scene appear surreal, as I inched closer to the bed where my husband lay, unconscious and covered with a sheet. I strained to see his face, but the doctors were in my way. "Let me see him," I cried, as a chorus of voices shouted, "Get her out of here! We're trying to save his life!"

The nurse pressed my arm as I followed her out of the room. All I could think was that if Norm was about to die, I had to see him one more time. *This can't be happening*, I thought, not even knowing what "this" was. I returned to the waiting room and sank into a chair, haunted by the inert body

I'd seen on the table. Rosie left at seven to meet the house full of people who would be arriving in an hour, while Ricardo and I tried to fill in the missing pieces. We just couldn't figure out what had happened. In half an hour or so, a nurse came out to say there was nothing I could do at the hospital. At Ricardo's urging, I decided to go back to the house and wait by the phone, but I dreaded facing a party atmosphere while my husband hovered between two worlds.

With swollen, red eyes, I entered Rosie's beautifully decorated house and went to hide in the kitchen next to the phone. A party held no draw for me at all, as I waited to hear whether Norm would live or die. At one point, I walked into the living room and took a seat next to Anthony, a dear friend of Norm's, who held my hand and told me a story about his son who had survived a car accident and a coma. The fact that his son was a college graduate and happily married comforted me. Anthony's soft voice and tender touch helped me get through a terrible ordeal, and I feel eternally bonded with this wonderful man.

I called the hospital again and again that night, but there was no news. When the doorbell rang at 9:30 P.M. and Frank arrived at the house, I jumped up from the kitchen stool, grabbed hold of him, and refused to let go. Sobbing in my son's arms, I thanked God that I had someone I loved to lean on.

After midnight, when the party was breaking up, Frank and I drove over to the hospital to see if we could get some information. We waited several hours, but there was no news. At about 4 A.M., we headed back to the hotel so I could shower and check out. Since family was arriving, I'd reserved several rooms at the Holiday Inn a few blocks from the hospital. I let the water rush over my body, trying to feel something — anything. I was numb, and couldn't even cry — until I started packing up Norm's and my suitcases and caught sight of the undelivered birthday gift Norm had been so excited about.

My tears flowed freely as I wheeled our suitcases to the elevator, thinking that when our friends listened to their answering machine, they would be receiving two messages in a row from us. The first would be Norm wishing them Happy New Year; the next would tell them that he had been in a terrible accident and nobody knew if he would make it. I stepped into the elevator wondering if Norm would ever have a chance to give the training wheels to his friend.

Chapter Four

Coma

Your Name Is Norm

"Your name is Norm Camp and mine is Dora. We're married." I repeated these words over and over, hoping Norm could hear me, even though his eyes were closed. "You've been in a serious bike accident," I told him, holding his hand, telling him how much I loved him, and trying to explain what had happened.

I was still in party clothes, sitting at Norm's bedside in the Intensive Care Unit of Scripps Encinitas Hospital. He was in a coma, hooked up to life-saving machines. A ventilator tube had been inserted in his trachea, helping him breathe. There were needles in his arms, hands, and throat, due to a condition called anoxic encephalopathy, a brain injury caused by oxygen deprivation to the brain tissues. I hate to imagine how bad it would have been if the paramedics hadn't arrived as quickly as they did. But if Norm died, none of that would matter.

I rushed out of Intensive Care and grabbed a nurse several times in that first hour, reporting that Norm had twitched an eye or moved a hand. I wanted each of these things to mean something, but they didn't. These kinds of involuntary movements were normal, they told me, when someone is in a coma; unless he moved as a result of a direct request, they were insignificant. Brain-stem reflexes at this point, however, *would* be significant.

I refused to believe them, certain that Norm could hear me and sense my presence. It was hard to fathom that he was as out of it as he seemed after a two-second fall, but he showed no signs of life. He'd broken four ribs and his clavicle, as well as sustaining severe bruises and abrasions, leaving the left side of his face scraped to the bone. And that was only the external damage.

His brain injury, invisible and hard to pinpoint, was the real problem.

I refused to see my husband as a lost cause. I stared at Norm's bruised face as his midsection rose and fell with each ventilated breath. I wanted to know his every thought and feeling, and whether he was in pain. Did he have any warning before he fell? I needed to know that he could understand what I was saying, especially if I had to say goodbye. Was he choosing whether or not to live? I had no answers, only unanswered questions as I watched Norm fight for his life. If I said the right thing, could I influence him to stick around? If I said the wrong thing, could I cause him to check out?

I pondered these questions as family and friends scrambled their schedules to arrive at the hospital. My stepson, John, was coming from the East Coast; stepdaughter Lindy was on her way from Lake Tahoe and would arrive the next day; Norm's brother, Gary, was flying in from Florida, and my good friend, Susan, was arriving from the Bay Area to help.

The Vigil

I put everyone up at the Holiday Inn, located one freeway exit from the hospital. We fell into a routine, leaving the inn each morning, piling into the car, and arriving at our home away from home — Scripps Encinitas Hospital. On the first day, the doctors reported that nothing had changed. Norm was in a coma and couldn't communicate with us; still, we never left him alone. Since ICU rules clearly stated that only two people were allowed at Norm's bedside at any one time, we alternated.

The bruises, which looked so terrible, were not causing him pain. They were the easy part, the doctors said, because they would heal. The damage to his brain was the question, because no one knew yet how much damage he had sustained, or whether the healing would happen. I talked to Norm, held his hand, and told him I loved him, hoping against hope for a response of any sort, but day one passed and Norm remained the same.

On day two, the doctor was not hopeful. I stayed by Norm's side anyway, leaving the room only when someone else took my place. What if Norm woke up and no one was there to explain what had happened? But after five days of the vigil with no response from Norm, the neurologist called a family meeting. Apparently, the medical staff had exhausted their cardiac protocols, and there was nothing left to do. We needed to share our love with Norm, the surgeon told us, and let nature take its course.

I understood the concept, but why not help nature along a little bit? I brought Norm a cassette of country and western, his favorite kind of music, and played it for him as I sang along. I felt kind of silly singing Western ballads to my sleeping husband, but I did it anyway. Hell, I'd have brought in a five-piece band if I could have gotten them into ICU. Frank tied a colorful balloon to the frame of Norm's bed, while I rubbed the uninjured parts of his battered body with massage creams and lotions, hoping the combination of the music, the color, people's motion, the massaging, and my constant appeals to him to wake up would do something. But we got no reaction whatsoever, not even when Norm's friend, Grant, stood at the foot of his bed and sang. There was tremendous pain and beauty in his song, as he and Norm had been close friends for many years, but nothing was working.

I finally arranged for a priest to visit Norm, so we could all pray together — until John, Norm's son, stopped us with a concern. What if his father awoke in the middle of the prayers, saw the priest, and thought he was dead? The priest accommodated us by turning his collar back to front, so Norm wouldn't see it. Then we formed a circle in his room, held hands, and prayed for him to wake up. And still, Norm remained motionless.

Each night when we left the hospital, we all met in one of our Holiday Inn rooms to talk. These nightly sessions were a great survival technique — a tremendous release for our emotions and frustrations. One night, for example, Norm's brother, John, who is a nurse, told us a story about a patient he had in a Florida ICU. The patient's highly superstitious family believed that if they waved a live chicken over their loved one, then took it to the ocean and released it into the waters, the illness would leave their sick family member. The staff agreed, he said, and the chicken feathers flew. We ended up laughing hysterically, a rare occurrence during that time.

I spent one evening telling everyone about Norm's connection to the Boy Scouts of America. He had joined the scouting program at age eleven, in 1951, and later became a summer-camp counselor. Norm had told so many stories about his scouting adventures, crediting his scout training and his scoutmaster, a man named Ed, for his public speaking ability and his love of leading people in their tasks.

Years later, in August 1954, when Norm was fourteen, having earned a grand total of twenty-one merit badges, he'd received his Eagle Scout Badge, of which he was very proud. He learned the merits of citizenship in the Boy Scouts, as well as first aid, cooking, camping, and American Indian laws, which he in turn taught the scouts he trained. As usual, Norm became one of their most respected trainers, taking on the job of training and supervising the work of the Eagle Scouts who followed in his footsteps.

When I broke out into a chorus of "The Worm Song," everyone had to hold their stomachs for fear of bursting with laughter. This was a song Norm had learned when he was a kid in camp. Now, as a testament to Norm's youthful personality even as an adult, I sang out the lyrics to one of his favorite childhood songs:

> Nobody likes me, everybody hates me, guess I'll go eat worms.
> Little ones, big ones, worms that turn and squirm.
> Everybody wonders how I eat them, three times every day.
> You bite off the heads, suck out the custard, and throw the skins away.

Although I cried a lot, it was good therapy to spend the nights talking about Norm and the multitude of his achievements. Often, I didn't get to sleep until 2 or 3 A.M, and then I was up early the next day to get to the hospital for another long day of the vigil. Those nightly "debriefings" were crucial to my emotional health and sanity.

We all did our best to stay positive during that week in hell, but I must admit that sometimes it didn't work. I remember the night when my stepdaughter Lindy and I admitted to each other that we weren't sure Norm would make it. We sobbed together, holding onto one another as I told her I hoped she would find the kind of love that Norm and I had. And then, the next day, the vigil started all over again.

Making Decisions

It was six days after the accident when I realized that I needed some fresh clothes. I'd been wearing the same two outfits I'd packed for the weekend, and there had to be mail and phone messages piling up back home. It was time for a quick break to drive home and take care of a few things. But the moment I arrived in La Crescenta, I got a phone call from ICU.

Norm had taken a turn for the worse and they were suggesting I come back immediately — these next hours might be his last.

I threw some clothes in the car, along with a pile of unopened mail, and sped back to San Diego in the pouring rain, tears streaming down my face. I still don't know how I made it. All I know is that I got Susan on the phone and I remember saying over and over, "I don't want him to die. He can't die. We love each other too much."

As soon as I arrived at the hospital, the neurologist, Doctor Brill, a kind, gentle man, called a family meeting. He stood at the front of a small room off the ICU, his back toward a chalkboard, trying to explain a situation that no one wanted to grasp. But denial was inappropriate right then, as he reminded us that Norm had been in a coma for seven days. They had determined that he had suffered a heart attack on his bike, which had caused his fall. In turn, the heart attack had reduced the amount of blood and oxygen to his brain for four to five minutes. As a result, Norm was diagnosed with "anoxia," oxygen deprivation to the brain, the worst kind of trauma, since no one had any idea which parts of his brain were affected.

Now we had a horrific decision to make — whether or not Norm should remain on life support. I cried when Doctor Brill said that he lifted Norm's eyelids and thought, "Behind those eyes there is a man trying to get out." That was Norm's tremendous will to live. I knew he wasn't ready to leave this earth, but I knew also that even if Norm awakened, he might be a vegetable. And, though we were all in the room as a family, the ultimate decision to let Norm live or die was mine.

I struggled with my emotions. As much as I selfishly wanted to keep Norm alive, I knew there was no way he would want to live in a vegetative state, which didn't seem like a life at all. I certainly wouldn't want it for myself in his place. But what if we decided to pull the plug ten minutes before he was getting ready to wake up and heal. I wouldn't wish this kind of life-and-death decision on anyone, but I separated myself from my emotions just enough to ask the right questions. When I learned that there was a hundred percent consensus among his doctors to remove him from life support, I did what I had to do: I agreed to take Norm off the electronic devices that were keeping him alive, knowing he would have wanted it that way.

I felt like I was in a trance as I started funeral arrangements for my husband who was still alive. I knew he would want to be buried in a naval cemetery, so, while the hospital staff began weaning him off the oxygen, I called one of his friends from the navy. The closest naval cemetery, I soon discovered, was in Riverside, California, but I went no further when I learned that Norm was tolerating the oxygen reduction and breathing on his own. I waited breathlessly while they removed the tubes from his throat, and wondered if I was seeing things when Norm woke up!

He was trying to talk, but his throat was too dry. I stared into his open eyes, wondering what I would do if he closed them again and died right in front of me. Had I made the right decision? What if his awakening had come too soon and he wasn't ready? Watching Norm fight his way back into consciousness, I made a pact with God: I'd take him in any condition at all and I'd figure out what to do next — if only he could come back to me in one piece.

Waking Up

Norm kept breathing, and eventually the family went their separate ways. I was sorry to see them leave, but now that the immediate danger was over, they had to get back to their lives. My dear son, Frank, who is self-employed, stayed with me as they moved Norm from ICU to a private room with a twenty-four-hour private nurse. Because the hospital was so close to several military bases in the San Diego area, military medics working part-time as hospital staff attended Norm. They showed a great deal of care and respect for him, even when he was doing crazy things like kicking his feet and throwing his arms around. I later found out that was an indication that Norm's brain was reconnecting with his body. At the time, however, it upset me terribly, and I wish someone would have told me that the thrashing was a sign of healing, not insanity.

We did everything we could to make Norm comfortable, padding his bed with blankets so he wouldn't hurt himself, tying him to his chair with sheets when we managed to sit him upright, and trying to understand what he was struggling to say. I took it one minute at a time, never thinking ahead, and ended up utterly exhausted every night. But I had my Norm back and would do everything in my power to help him regain his life.

We had our rough times, like when Norm kept asking to go to the bathroom, even though they had fitted him with a catheter. It seemed he had no idea what a catheter was and what it did, and insisted on being lifted to the bathroom time and again, where he just stood and stared. One of our best moments, though, was when Ricardo saw Norm sitting up in a chair. Ricardo had some inappropriate guilt, feeling he should have been able to do something. When Norm recognized his friend and spoke his name aloud, Ricardo was so relieved and grateful that he took the special ball cap, which he had received for outstanding achievement at work, off his own head and put it on Norm's.

All in all, Norm could not have received better care than he did at Scripps. The nurses and dedicated staff were supportive of Norm and our family, even when we didn't follow their rules. They did everything they could to make it easier on us, but on January 9, 1997, ten days after the accident, we faced our toughest problem to date: Norm had to check out of the hospital — and I had no idea what to do with him next.

Chapter Five

Starting Our Journey

The Long Journey Home

It didn't feel like we were going fast enough, but maybe that was because the siren wasn't letting out the piercing sound that warns everyone to stop. People stared at the ambulance anyway, as we sped along our hundred-mile journey from Scripps Encinitas to Midland Medical Center in Burbank. *Faster, faster,* was all I could think.

After nine nightmarish days, we were moving Norm, who had finally exhibited enough signs of stability to make the change safely — or so we hoped. He was far from what I would call "in good shape." His face had begun to heal, but his lips were gashed from the ventilator tube that had been down his throat for so long. He couldn't walk yet, and the scabs on his arms and legs were still deep and obvious. Since he hadn't been able to brush since the accident, his teeth were yellow. The doctors had replaced his intravenous feeding tube with a gastrostomy tube, which was surgically implanted through his abdominal wall, above his belly button, and directly into his stomach. He was having trouble with chronic restlessness, throwing his arms and legs around, and though he could speak some words and occasionally make short sentences, his brain wasn't transmitting to his vocal chords fast enough, causing him frustration with the hesitation in his speech patterns.

But the doctors felt that he could make the move, hopefully without suffering another heart attack, and I needed to get him closer to home. I watched them wheel Norm out on a gurney and load him into the back of the ambulance. He didn't fight at all; he just lay there and did what he was told, for which I was grateful and heartbroken at the same time. If he had fought the ambulance attendants, he could have strained his heart — but the fact that he didn't fight made it all the more obvious how badly he had been damaged.

It was my first time in an ambulance; I sat in the front seat, awed by the walkie-talkies and telephones built into the dashboard. In the back, the intravenous injection hookups and emergency heart-response equipment took up most of the space, though the nurse I'd hired had managed to squeeze herself in beside Norm. She continuously communicated with him: "Are you all right, Norm? Can you see me? Are you warm enough?" She pulled the blanket up to his chin. *Thank God she's here,* I thought. I prayed that Norm would survive the drive — the most I could hope for at the time.

I spent most of the trip staring at him. And there was Frank, devoted son, just behind us, following in his car. The nurse kept talking to Norm, informing him where we were and keeping his attention engaged. None of it made sense to him; I could see that nothing was registering in his eyes, but she was keeping his body still and soothing his mind. I listened and watched, feeling powerless but relieved that I could live at home throughout Norm's recovery.

At one point, his arms began flailing and the nurse talked him down. Had I made the wrong decision? Was he really ready for such a long drive, or had I jumped the gun? What would Norm have chosen for himself? There was no answer to that, I realized, or to any other questions concerning my husband. Norm, the man who had taken care of everything all the time, could no longer make the simplest decisions for me or himself or anyone else. It was apparent now that from here on, for better or worse, I would make all the decisions for both of us.

Terror seized me. I felt incapable at that moment of deciding what color socks to put on. How could I make life-determining choices for Norm when I had no idea what was going on in his head? It would take enormous discipline to accept this drastic, unwelcome change in our lifestyles. Norm and I had both been such independent people — one of the reasons our marriage had worked so well. Now, I would be the one deciding for Norm, making choices that might be different from those he would make for himself.

One moment at a time, I thought, pulling myself into the present. I spent most of the trip — the first hour and a half since the accident when I wasn't rushing around to handle and arrange things — waffling between states of denial and full awareness of the truth of the situation. Everything was happening so fast, I'd had no time to think. I stared behind me at the docile man lying on the gurney. This was not my husband, at least, not the husband with whom I'd lived for the past seven years. And I hadn't even had a chance to grieve my loss — I'd been much too busy.

As if nothing out of the ordinary were going on, I watched the scenery fly by. All of our family and friends, except for Frank, had gone home to resume their lives. After all, no one had died and Norm was getting better. But the old Norm *had* died from the life we'd lived before, and so had part of me. I was now married to a man who could do nothing for himself or for me. With no time at all to think of myself in weeks, I'd been snacking randomly on unhealthy foods. When I finally bothered to look in the mirror, I was shocked to see that my hair was flat and scraggly, my nails were broken, and I'd gained nearly fifty pounds. I looked as if I'd aged ten years, which made sense, since every time I'd tried to sleep, worries about money and our home and everything else had gone through my head until I was up again, pacing anxiously and making late-night raids on the refrigerator.

About halfway through the trip to Burbank, I remembered the moment when I'd first seen Norm lying comatose on the bed in the ICU. I had pled with God, "Give him back to me in any shape and I'll do whatever it takes." God had made good on His side of the bargain, but between making sure Norm got the care he needed and acting as his advocate for recovery, there was no place left to be his wife. I only hoped that Norm's internist, who practiced at Midland Medical Center in Burbank where we were headed, would help me with some important decisions, such as whether it was the right place for a person with brain injury. I hadn't had time to do the research, but I knew that the staff would make all the difference.

Hospital Hell

When we finally exited the Hollywood Freeway, we circled the block and pulled up at the emergency entrance of Midland Medical. Paramedics and the nurse opened the back doors of the ambulance and carried Norm out on the gurney and into the hallway. Then the nurse went straight to the admitting desk, where we faced our first challenge. Although Scripps had contacted Midland, they'd forgotten to confirm Norm's arrival. As a result, his insurance company had not okayed his admission, and there was no bed for him. He was admitted to the Transitional Care Unit, pending evaluation of improvement for transfer to Acute Rehabilitation.

This took nearly an hour to sort out, during which Norm was becoming restless on the gurney. His nurse, my hero at that moment, spoke up in a firm voice, telling the staff that they'd better do something soon or there'd be hell to pay. He was admitted to the Transitional Care Unit, and within twenty-four hours was transferred to the Acute Rehabilitation floor.

I felt relieved, but soon discovered that only one other patient on the floor had sustained brain injury, and he'd been there six months. The rest were recovering from hip or knee replacements. My worst fear was realized when I saw that Norm was in a facility whose staff had no experience with brain-injured people. The hospital had no special units or programs that would benefit him. Even Glenda, our caseworker on the Acute Rehabilitation floor, had no idea how to treat Norm.

For starters, the nurses weren't interacting with him skillfully, telling him nothing about the various procedures he was undergoing. He got upset each time they approached him with a needle or a thermometer — and why wouldn't he? He wasn't an idiot; he was brain-injured, which apparently meant the same thing to the uniformed staff.

When we first arrived, they acquainted me with the therapy scheduling board, but on many days that Norm was scheduled for therapy, no one ever came and got him. Often, I'd arrive at the hospital to find Norm so sedated and groggy that he couldn't perform the simplest tasks that were expected of him, like sitting up and feeding himself.

Eventually, Frank and I asked for a bed in Norm's room so we could be with him around the clock, dividing the time between us. It seemed that when one of us was there, Norm was never irritated or upset, but any time he was left alone, he would act up. Knowing something was wrong, I pondered what to do while watching them begin teaching Norm to walk. He learned quickly, and once he placed his feet on the floor and propelled himself around with the footrest of his wheelchair lifted up, he refused to allow it to be down ever again. It was quite a sight to see Norm in his wheelchair, and Frank in another wheelchair close behind, motoring around the hospital unit together.

As grateful as we were for his progress, once Norm had mastered the act of walking on his own, we had a new set of problems. The part of Norm's brain that told him when to sleep had been damaged, and he walked the halls day and night. Midland wasn't equipped to handle his individual needs, nor were they thrilled to have Frank and me there all the time. But whenever Norm was alone, they resorted to sedating him — against our wishes — to keep him quiet. The sedation only made him angry and groggy, and he walked the halls all night long anyway, until he collapsed in the hallway where a nurse would rush to pick him up, take him back to his room, and help him lie down.

Norm tried to relax, but within seconds he was up and walking again, a behavior he had no control over. I wore wrinkle-free clothing so I could get in and out of bed with him and accompany him on his endless walks from nowhere to nowhere. While we walked, he would ask me, "How many houses do I own? How many cars do I own?" His questions made no sense; he didn't know his name or what had happened to him. I answered him anyway, aware that he had no ability to do anything with the information. Once when we were walking he asked me to have a drink with him. We stopped at a window, and when I pointed out a miniature golf course across the street, he said, "Well, there won't be any bars around here."

One morning when I was still up from the night before, Frank took over my shift. I arrived home thinking about a hot shower and a moment to look through the ever-growing stacks of unopened mail, when the phone rang. It was the hospital, telling me Norm was out of control and I had to come right back. It seemed that they had tried to take his temperature rectally, without explaining it to him. Not understanding what they were doing, he had defended himself. That sounded pretty healthy to me, since they had come at him aggressively without making him feel safe first. The staff treated him as if he were mentally retarded, not brain-injured, two conditions that had nothing whatsoever to do with each other, but try telling that to an overworked and underpaid nurse who hadn't been trained in acquired brain injury (ABI).

I hurried back to the hospital, wondering how on earth they could treat a human being that way. Even I, in a very short time, had learned that Norm needed to be told what was going on each step of the way. This incident was one more demonstration that brain-injured people need to have specially trained staff. Putting them in with the general population of patients does not produce a healing environment, and in Norm's case, it was causing him to backslide.

After I got Norm straightened out, Glenda, our nurse and family friend, took me aside, looked into my tired eyes and said, "You're being too optimistic about your husband's recovery."

Glenda's attitude was hard to understand, because she and her family had been to our home and attended social events together. She knew how smart Norm was and she knew his potential. Why couldn't she be adaptable and work with me? I looked right back at her and declared, "Norm will be skiing this season."

I might have been kidding myself but I needed hope and some goals. Glenda argued for a moment, suggesting I needed to be more realistic, but I refused to see things her way. When I returned to Norm's room, I knew we needed to make other arrangements for this phase of his recovery.

A few days later, when I returned to the hospital after a short nap, I found my husband tied to his bed, restraints on his hands, feet, and neck. The neck restraint was so tight that his face was turning redder with his every effort to free himself. I had expressly forbidden them to use restraints, and this was the last straw. "What the hell are you doing to him?" I yelled at the nurse standing next to me. I could hear myself screaming as I untied the restraint from his left hand and then his left leg. As I rounded the end of the bed to get to his right hand I yelled, "Get the head nurse in here and call Doctor Spiral, head of the department and Norm's internist."

My shouting brought several nurses into the room to see what was happening. "Who gave you permission to put my husband in restraints?" I blustered at them.

"He was becoming a threat and we were afraid for our safety," one of them said, trying to calm me down as I continued undoing the ties. At this point, Norm was composed, just watching what was going on as I started to take off his pajamas and put on his shirt and pants, quietly explaining to him what I was doing and what I expected him to do. He didn't appear to be upset at what had just happened, thank goodness. Maybe he'd already forgotten, but I hadn't. After I had him dressed, I bounded out of the room and into the nurse's station just across the hall.

"I'm checking my husband out right now before you people kill him," I told them.

"You can't take him until he's released," a nurse said. "Something might happen to him at home."

"Nothing could be worse than what's happening to him here. He's a lot safer at home where we understand that this man has a brain injury. I demand to speak with both of his doctors."

Norm's internist was out of town, but they reached Doctor Spiral, head of the Acute Rehabilitation Department. I grabbed the phone and told Doctor Spiral what had happened. He felt that Norm wasn't ready to go home, and he assured me that they would never touch him again without first getting my approval, but I didn't believe him. I relaxed only after he gave me his personal cell-phone number, telling me to contact him if anything else happened.

Our eventual agreement was that either Frank or I would be in Norm's room twenty-four hours a day, with the door closed and a table against it. That way, Norm couldn't get out — and the nurses couldn't get in — unless one of us opened the door. In the meantime, private nurses were called in daily, but there were problems there, too. Norm, who was still walking the halls all day and night, was given a private nurse whose bunions were so big and painful that she couldn't walk beside him. Finally, a kind, caring, efficient woman named Aurora was assigned to Norm during the day, and she walked with him patiently and lovingly. We were not so lucky with the night nurse, however, since different ones came each night, and sometimes no one showed up at all.

Norm's first male night nurse upset him so much that Norm was forced into defense mode. When they called us in the middle of the night and we rushed to the hospital, we found two security guards holding Norm down while he fought for his life — all because the nurse wanted Norm to change into his pajamas. When Frank, my gentle giant, firmly told the guards to unhand Norm or they wouldn't live to see the next day, they believed him and released Norm. They left the room with assurances from Frank that he would press charges if he ever saw them in Norm's room again.

I demanded to know why such things never happened when we were there, or when Norm was with tiny Aurora, who weighed about ninety-eight pounds. The office personnel answered that their staff had not been trained to handle a person with brain injury. They promised they would see to it that they got training from now on, but we never found a nurse other than Aurora who understood how to handle Norm. I knew the additional trauma they were causing him was counterproductive to his recovery. We had to move him, but where and when?

Moving Norm Again

Glenda gave me a ton of literature on convalescent homes, but I refused to go that route. Did she think I would check Norm into a home where he could vegetate, holding a TV remote until he died? Out of the question! Glenda was a smart woman, but she had a lot to learn about brain injury.

Doctor Spiral felt that Norm would benefit from a more structured environment such as acute rehabilitation. There, he could learn to better deal with his cognitive and behavioral issues in addition to progressing with mobility and self-care activities. Once again I was at odds with the doctor's suggestions: I believed Norm needed to be in an environment where he'd be stimulated to relearn some of his basic skills, like writing, reading, and signing his name. Doctor Spiral also thought that the family would need to have training prior to his discharge; I couldn't help thinking it was the other way around — the family could train the hospital staff!

Norm's brother, Gary, an RN in Florida, checked the Internet for places that handled ABI. After long talks with various hospital staffs, Gary found a place called Casa Colina, which was only sixty miles from home. Doctor Spiral and several nurses said that this facility had an excellent reputation for ABI care, so I scheduled an appointment for a tour of the premises. Unfortunately, on the day of our appointment, the Midland Medical Center had failed to hire a nurse to be with Norm. I couldn't risk leaving him alone, so I stayed with Norm while the children, Lindy and Frank, checked out Casa Colina.

They returned, impressed with the facility. They were emotional about the fact that their dad needed to be admitted to a brain-trauma center, but they felt that the place and its highly trained staff could really help Norm, and they told him so. Norm listened, but had no idea what was about to happen to him. Once again, it was up to me to make the hard choices. I hated the fact that my husband and I couldn't discuss such an important decision that would affect both of our lives. I missed having someone to bounce ideas off of, but it was up to me, and I decided to go forward.

The first step to admitting Norm to the brain-trauma center was an interview with Doctor Morris, director of Casa Colina. He arrived at the hospital that very evening, looked over Norm's records, and interviewed me. Norm watched carefully, studying my reaction to this strange man sitting on his bed. Doctor Morris was impressed that Norm's attention span was so good. When he said that he felt they could help Norm, and agreed to admit him to Casa Colina, I nearly cried with joy. Finally, someone was saying something positive about Norm's condition and his future.

So, fifteen days after Norm arrived at Midland Medical, a group of us stood by the ambulance entrance for the move to Casa Colina, where he would become a resident for the next three months. Ironically, when Norm stood with the rest of us, preparing to get on the gurney, it took the paramedics a moment to figure out who was the patient. When there are no outside signs or scars with brain injury, it is difficult for an outsider to believe that something is wrong. If the paramedics had trouble distinguishing a brain-injured person from a healthy one, we were in for some huge challenges. But we would do this thing one step at a time, and getting Norm into the hospital was the task at hand.

What a relief that he was going to a place where people would understand why he was acting in certain ways and what to do with him. I could rest a little easier knowing he'd no longer be abused. I'd anticipated that the move wouldn't be easy, but once it was over and Norm was safe and sound in Casa Colina, I could breathe again.

Not that I expected to get my life back, I knew better than that, but I looked forward to not being in a hospital twenty-four hours every day. Just knowing Norm would be in good hands made the trip to Casa Colina an exercise in hope — something caregivers of brain-injured loved ones have to fight for every day of their lives.

Chapter Six

The Right Place

Settling In

Casa Colina occupied several blocks of a sprawling campus-like facility. *It's so much larger than I'd expected,* I thought, as I passed a building with an outdoor playground full of gym equipment. I would learn later that they had a school on site for brain-injured children who were having trouble functioning in traditional settings.

The next turn revealed a suburban-looking two-story house. The ambulance driver told me this was the transitional living center (TLC), where Norm would be staying. I looked up at the darkening sky. It was only 5 P.M., and the light was nearly gone. It felt foreboding. How would Norm react to the change of residence? How would the staff relate to us? I prayed that Norm wouldn't be nervous, that he'd see this as different from the previous hospital.

The paramedics backed up the ambulance to the front porch. A few men were standing beside some empty chairs, watching us. One of them was smoking a cigarette. They looked so fit and well dressed that I had no idea if they were staff or residents. Frank and I went to the back door of the ambulance to oversee them moving the gurney Norm was on. He grinned broadly when he recognized Frank. I leaned against my son's strong body for support. As much as we needed to be at Casa Colina, I hated the thought of leaving Norm in this place or anywhere else, but I surely couldn't handle him by myself, since he was still walking nearly twenty-four hours a day and couldn't groom himself.

As they rolled Norm through the front door, the men on the porch began whispering among themselves. I greeted them with a smile and they smiled back. We entered a large room with a massive stone fireplace and couches arranged to face the colorful, warming blaze. A long table strewn with books and a lamp created a cozy reading area. To the far right was the glassed-in staff station, where they could see everything going on in the living room. Amateur paintings covered the walls (done by the residents?), and to our left was a dining room with a large wooden country-style table and chairs. I sighed with relief. After the sterile hospital environment we'd just left, this place felt warm and inviting. Norm would like it here.

I wandered into the kitchen, which looked as much like a home setting as possible, designed to make it easier for people to transition back to their homes when the time came. I hoped it wouldn't be too long for Norm. In that kitchen, the staff taught the residents to prepare and cook food, and, with the help of the staff, residents could raid the fridge when they wanted a snack.

Adjoining the kitchen was a den, a comfortable room with a big-screen TV and soft couches. This was where residents would gather in the mornings, as the staff encouraged them to watch the news and reconnect with the outside world. Two side tables were covered with magazines and newspapers, reminding me of a ski chalet. The residents who were seated in the various rooms seemed content, which was very important to me.

Katherine, the TLC director, a middle-aged woman dressed in business clothes, approached us and greeted Norm personally. "How was your ride here from Burbank?" she asked him. He didn't answer; he really didn't understand what was going on, but he responded pleasantly to her smile and her comforting demeanor. Although I was devastated that Norm was unable to respond, it was wonderful to see Katherine treating him like a human being. She led us on a tour of the rooms, introducing us to everyone we encountered along the way. Some of them had obvious disabilities, like difficulty with walking and talking; some were in wheelchairs, and others seemed entirely normal. Everyone was pleasant, and some told Norm they were happy he was there.

I hesitated at the doorway of a room that was to be Norm's home for the next ninety days. Picture windows rose on one side, allowing us to see neighboring homes across the street. There were two twin beds, though Norm would have the room to himself, and there was a sink with a mirror and several drawers for Norm's shorts, socks, tee shirts, and warm clothes.

To the left of the sink was a long closet, big enough to hold Norm's hang-up clothing. Katherine said we could customize the room to his taste, but, as with any other institution, no pictures were allowed on the walls, and no food in the rooms, to discourage ants and other unwelcome critters.

In all, the room was nice and clean and the place was welcoming, yet I hated thinking of Norm staying here, a stranger in a place full of strangers. I yearned for the not so distant past, when Norm and I would climb into bed, lie back on the down pillows, pull up the comforter, and hold one another, safe in each other's arms. Things had changed drastically in a month, and today, I was getting a pretty good dose of how my life had been and would continue to be impacted by ABI.

Clinton, a short, stocky black man in his early thirties, entered Norm's room. I liked him right away as he beamed a contagious smile. For the first few nights, he assured us, he would be sitting outside Norm's room while he slept, making sure he was safe. I appreciated Clinton's soft, gentle way, and he seemed very good with Norm, asking him questions and trying to get a conversation going. Norm stayed close to me. It seemed that as long as he could see me, he was okay, but if I tried to leave for even a minute, he wanted to come with me. How could I tell him that I was going home while he had to stay here? I just didn't know how I'd endure my own departure.

I forced my attention to the task at hand, sorting Norm's clothing. All we had were the bare necessities: pajamas, shorts, shirts, pants, socks, and shoes. *I'll bring more tomorrow,* I thought, as I used a black marker to scrawl his initials on each article of clothing. Norm looked confused by the activity, but he stayed still while I finished marking his clothes and putting them into the drawers. It all seemed surreal; I never imagined I'd be doing this for my husband. Our lives and my role in our marriage were changed forever; and I hated every bit of it, but I could do nothing to change it, and Norm needed a chance at a better life. Casa Colina just might be the place that could make it happen.

It had been a long day, and the sky was dark when Frank left to return to Big Bear. I hugged him goodbye with wet eyes, and called our friends, the Parkers, to pick me up. I stared at my husband, walking up and down the halls, unable to sleep, eat, dress himself, use the facilities, or communicate in a meaningful way. Settling him into the TV room, I sat beside him, wondering how to break the news that I was leaving for the night. We struck up conversations with other residents who were also watching TV. Norm tried to communicate, but the words wouldn't come out. He looked frustrated, but seemed content as long as I was there.

When the time approached for me to leave, the staff began to distract Norm with books and games. They lured him into the recreation room and he followed without making a fuss. They stopped at a pool table, inviting Norm to give it a try, while I sneaked out without saying goodbye. I left a part of my heart behind, feeling like I was abandoning my husband in his most vulnerable hour. As soon as the front door closed behind me, tears rolled down my cheeks. As the Parkers drove me away, I questioned whether I was doing the right thing. Silently, I pleaded, *Please, God, just keep him safe until tomorrow morning.*

An Empty House

H ome felt like death itself. The yard needed cleaning, the flowers were dead, and dust covered every surface. There were no signs of life, and I had no energy to do a thing about it. All I wanted was for the night to speed by so I could get back to Casa Colina. Climbing into bed was a relief, but my overactive mind allowed me only two hours of sleep, even when I used the tried-and-true system I call "self-talk" to get through a long, hard night.

I can't remember when I haven't used self-talk, but with Norm's illness, it helped me stay sane. It calms me and helps me use my imagination, a skill crucial to dealing with ABI. For example, when I decided that Norm needed to be at Casa Colina, self-talk — talking to myself as if this were a business decision rather than an emotional issue — helped me find the fastest and simplest way to get it done.

This night, as much as I wanted to put Norm in the car with me, I knew he had to stay where he was, for the good of both of us. "He's better off here," I repeated with as little emotion as possible. When I couldn't sleep, I told myself, "Dora, if you don't get some rest, you won't be healthy enough to take care of either of you. And if something happens to you, who'll care for Norm?" It was like an argument with myself going on in my head, and I had to win.

Finally, I managed to drop off to sleep, but awoke before the sun was up, too much information and too many questions spinning in my head. How would we survive? Was I doing the right thing? How would I pay the bills? Was Norm going to die? In desperation I resorted to QVC, the Cable shopping channel, which, thank goodness, had twenty-four-hour programming; I focused on a diamond baguette ring with emeralds, and a brooch that looked like a sparkling snowflake.

The sun rose as I brewed a fresh pot of coffee. I inhaled the aroma, trying to remember the last time I'd watched the sunrise. I stood on the back deck listening to the birds sing. Squirrels hurried across tree branches, jumping to the earth below to find food. I sipped my coffee. Life went on, no matter what was happening in it.

I sat for a few minutes, staring out over the houses below. In the distance, the sun reflected off the glass sides of the buildings in downtown Los Angeles, producing a blinding light. I could have stayed there all day, but I bounded out of my chair as anxiety settled in my chest. How could I sit here, relaxing and enjoying the morning, when I had no idea how Norm was feeling? I had to get to Casa Colina and see how he had done during his first night. I chose a few of Norm's colorful golf sweaters and some of his favorite sports shirts. Maybe his favorite clothes would give him a pick-me-up — if he remembered they were his and that he had once liked them.

By the time I had packed up his clothes, I couldn't get my own on fast enough. Why was I still at home? Had Norm walked all night and disturbed everyone? Would the staff know it wasn't his fault, that he had no control over his actions? Once dressed, I grabbed a few more pairs of Norm's shorts, pants, and socks, stuffed them in a black suitcase, and jumped into the car to begin the sixty-mile drive that would soon feel like second nature. Savoring the cool breeze on my face as I drove, I felt hopeful for the first time in a month. Maybe we were on the right road — if nothing disastrous had happened overnight!

Trouble in Paradise

Norm was in the main room when I arrived, dressed and ready to go — nowhere. He looked clean and rested, and when he saw me, he walked very quickly toward me, his hands extended to hug me. But where were his glasses? And what was that small cut over his eye? I glanced swiftly around the room, but no staff member was present to explain how Norm got cut. I went into instantaneous protective mode, flashing back to his mistreatment in the facility we had left the day before. Was it happening again? Where was Clinton, who was supposed to have watched over Norm all night?

I demanded some quick answers, but Clinton had gone home to sleep, and no one seemed to know what had happened. One look at my face told the staff they'd better come up with an explanation, and soon. Not five minutes had passed when a male nurse showed up to look at Norm's eye. He applied first aid to the cut. My anger continued escalating. Norm was supposed to start school today, and what had happened to his face and his glasses?

Finally, someone found his glasses under his bed, smashed, as if they'd been stepped on. I never did find out what had occurred, but surmised that Norm had gotten up in the night, dropped his glasses while trying to put them on, and then stepped on them. He showed no other signs of having been mistreated, but my antennae were up. Norm needed me as his advocate more than ever, since people with ABI are so vulnerable to being taken advantage of. When it happens, they can't defend themselves, and usually can't even remember what happened long enough to report it.

A staff member soothed me, saying that Norm had gotten out of bed by himself during the night, walked around, and sat down to watch TV. And he had slept two whole hours — more than he'd slept since coming out of his coma. Obviously, it agreed with him to be left alone to wander without restriction, and it wasn't dangerous, since this was all safe territory, with Clinton watching from far enough away not to annoy him or get in his way. I dared to hope that this, despite the broken glasses, was the beginning of Norm's healing.

I needed to get Norm a new pair of glasses, which, under normal circumstances, would have been a routine appointment, but nothing was routine anymore. I chose a strong titanium frame that would resist abuse, and shatterproof plastic lenses. But how could I get Norm's prescription? He wasn't able to handle himself in public yet, so I scoured the *Yellow Pages* for an optometrist in the neighboring town of La Verne.

I explained the situation to a kind attendant on the phone. "I'd appreciate any ideas you have to help me get this done." I was quickly learning to ask for help, something I continue doing to this day. They went out of their way, calling Norm's regular optometrist for his prescription, and the technician even agreed to go to TLC and measure Norm's eyes — more than I had dared hope for. He assured me that Norm would have his new glasses in a couple of days. I was relieved, but, having no guarantee that the breakage wouldn't happen again, I bought the one-year replacement policy. When it was all done, I sat back for a moment to breathe. Norm would be able to attend class and start relearning his reading skills in just a few days.

Chapter Seven

Reclaiming Knowledge

Meeting John

C asa Colina was working out. Each day, Norm greeted me with a big smile on his face; no more cuts or broken glasses. At the end of the day, he didn't seem to mind my leaving, but always asked when I would be back. He often called me at home, since he had access to a phone, and the staff would help him dial our number. I felt better knowing that Norm could reach me whenever he wanted to, and he felt less out of control because there were people there to help.

I had a little hope, but now that Norm had his glasses and could start school, I dreaded learning the real extent of his brain injury. We walked together off to the right of the large sitting room, outside, and across a lush lawn. The aroma of blooming roses mingled with the scent of fresh-mowed grass as we prepared to enter the classroom. It was time for another dose of reality that I wasn't ready, for, but then, I never would be, so now was as good a time as any.

On the lawn, just outside the glass doors to the classroom, we passed a small round table with four chairs and an umbrella. An alternative for good weather, perhaps. When we entered the classroom, I shaded my eyes a moment against the bright light that poured through the curtainless windows. Three rows of tables with folding chairs beside them faced the front of the room. A large chalkboard and a teacher's desk faced the tables, while students' hand-drawn pictures of sports heroes, sailing boats, and ocean scenes covered the walls.

In a moment, a gentleman in a wheelchair came rolling toward us, smiling. It was John, Norm's speech therapist, who had contracted polio when he was young. He had been walking, but we found out later that he began using the wheelchair for fear that he might fall and break a leg or a hip. He welcomed us, inviting Norm and me to sit at a table, while he wheeled himself around to sit on the other side facing us.

This session was to be one-on-one, as John explained that he was about to test Norm's memory, his ability to understand directions, his ability to follow instructions, and several other tests. Once the results were in, he'd know where Norm needed to begin. Inwardly, I cringed at realizing that my husband, with his Ph.D., his genius mind, and his advanced mathematical skills, was back to square one, and we had no idea how far back square one was.

John began a test, only to find that Norm could only stay awake for six seconds at a time. Then he would slump down in his chair, his head on the table. John would maneuver himself around the table and stop Norm from falling out of the chair. I watched this man in awe — someone who was facing so many challenges, yet wanted to help others get their lives back.

Every little sound and motion in the room distracted Norm. If someone walked by the door, Norm's attention was drawn away from the testing, and then he fell asleep. John quickly determined that we needed privacy, suggesting we adjourn to a room with a door that John could close. This very small room, just off the main classroom, had a table and three chairs crowded into it, and no space to spare.

Norm sat on the far side of the table, I sat against the wall, and John sat facing Norm and asking him questions:

"What is your daughter's name?"

"Where were you born?"

"How old are you?"

"Who is the President of the United States?"

"Do you know where you are?"

Norm couldn't answer one question, which triggered a few terrible questions of my own.

Was his brain as damaged as it seemed to be?

Was there any hope for him to lead an independent life?

While seeing Norm's mind unsuccessfully grappling with questions that meant nothing to him, I faced the reality of the uphill climb confronting us. The worst part was having no idea whether or how we would ever make it to the top.

At one point, John told Norm that he was hiding a key under a pile of books behind him. When a timer went off, Norm was supposed to tell John it was time to end the session and where the key was hidden. But when the timer went off, Norm looked around questioningly and the session was over. There was no denying the severity of Norm's condition — it was right there in front of my face.

We walked back to the main room, where a staff member who was setting the table invited me to stay for dinner. When they placed Norm's tray in front of him, I was horrified to see that he couldn't figure out how to remove the plastic wrap from a glass of milk. He couldn't get the top off the small tub of butter, either, and started stabbing the butter with a fork and trying to drink the milk through the plastic.

As if that weren't enough, I watched miserably while Norm tried to cut his hamburger. Finally, when he couldn't figure out how to use the fork or spoon, he shoved the burger into his mouth with his hands. A patient staff member tried to remedy the situation by putting Norm's food back on the plate and putting the silverware back into his hands. I knew they were trying to help him learn to eat again, but I was concerned about the lack of food and drink he was getting, and feared that he might never be able to feed himself.

I was relieved that the day was coming to a close when Norm and I pushed away from the table and sat quietly next to each other in the TV room. At 9 P.M., I told Norm I had to leave. I kissed him, telling him I'd see him early the next morning, and headed home exhausted, hoping that I could get some sleep. At least I felt comfortable leaving Norm for the night, but I wondered how I'd make it through tomorrow.

Progress

We had our first bit of good news the next day: Norm had slept four hours in a row (an hour more than I had), and the entire staff was excited. This was more rest than he'd gotten since the heart attack. I felt optimistic. Two nights ago, he had logged two hours, and now four. He was getting better.

When Jane, one of the occupational therapists, told me they were planning a trip to a local museum on the coming Saturday, we all wondered if Norm would be well enough to go. He surprised us all by starting to sleep through the night, and Jane told me on Friday that she felt Norm could go on the outing. She felt it would be good for Frank and me, too, because we could start learning how to handle the different situations that might arise once Norm was out in the real world. For now, if he fell, or behaved inappropriately, Jane would be there to get us through it, but we needed to know how to cope with whatever the future would bring.

That Saturday morning, when I arrived at Casa Colina, Norm was excited. He really didn't know what was scheduled for the day, and didn't understand what was happening, but he could sense the excitement, as everyone was talking fast and moving around. Frank drove down from Big Bear, and a group of us got into Jane's van and headed to the museum. I whispered to Frank, "Just think, four days ago, the doctors at Midland wanted to put Norm in a home." And here we were, going to visit a museum!

As we toured the museum, Jane pointed out objects of interest. "This rock is over 400 years old," she told everyone. Norm stood quietly, not listening. It appeared that nothing anyone said registered in his brain, but he had no trouble being there and seemed to enjoy the outing. I continued to marvel at the life sentence Norm's doctors had declared for him. What would they think now to see him sleeping through the night, showering, dressing, brushing his teeth, and well on his way to recovery? This was a very important day for both Frank and me. Having battled for so long to keep Norm functional without any tangible results, we were now getting a glimpse of the brass ring and we were ready to do whatever was necessary to grasp it.

On our way home from the museum we stopped for a bite at a local hamburger stand. Jane was afraid Norm was still incapable of handling a crowd or holding on to a hamburger well enough to get it in his mouth, but when we pleaded with her, she gave in. Triumphantly, I ordered a burger for Norm. He had a hard time figuring out what to do with the paper wrapping, but we showed him how to remove it and he managed to get it in his mouth. Success! He liked what he was tasting. In the end, he made a bigger mess than most, but the notion that he could tell the difference between institution food and other food was huge progress.

It seemed, however, that with each step forward, there was a step back, and dealing with food was no exception. Norm had lost a lot of weight while in a coma, shrinking from size 36 pants to 29, but as soon as he realized how good food tasted outside of Casa Colina, all he wanted to do was eat — at McDonald's, of all places. He liked a few of the local eateries, but each time Frank would come by to take him to lunch, Norm insisted on going to the golden arches, where he would scarf as much as he could.

The trouble was, due to his short-term memory loss, he'd forget when he'd last eaten, and he started gaining back his weight — and then some. But he continued to show progress, got better at taking a shower, and always wore a nice shirt and sweater. The staff waited each day to see what he would put on, and they enjoyed the character and color of his wardrobe. In the meantime, Norm had gathered enough strength and physical range of motion to take walks instead of stumbling along the corridors. His depth perception was still poor, and he was bad at opening cartons or sugar packets when eating, but he *was* eating and drinking, and a few things were beginning to make sense to him.

The truth was that Norm still needed moderate assistance with most activities, but he'd quickly learned to do most self-care tasks, like undressing and dressing. The hardest part was his difficulty with sequencing, a common problem among those with ABI. Whether to put on the socks or shoes first was a dilemma, the kind he faced in so many areas of his life. Nonetheless, he was learning things, slowly but surely, and I tried to stay focused on how far he'd come, rather than how far he still had to go.

The day that his therapists thought he was ready to attend class with other students, I was by his side, learning how to teach him the simplest things. John would ask the class, "What is the capital of California and who is governor?" He'd discuss current events with his students each morning, as Norm tackled the list of about thirty things he needed to relearn. They'd ask him the same questions at least three times a day, until he started getting some of the answers: "What are you children's names? Where do you live? What is your telephone number? What is your wife's name?"

Even though he'd answer a random question now and then, Norm wasn't interested in participating in class. He never raised his hand to answer a question, and he seemed bored as he sat staring into space until John forced him to talk. Poor Norm had lost his self-confidence, having embarrassed himself so many times by trying to talk and finding no words, but one day, he surprised us all. The class was planning a picnic at a nearby park, and deciding on a date, time, and mode of transportation. As usual, Norm remained quiet and disinterested — until the topic of food arose. When someone suggested they get nonfat ice cream because certain people had diabetes, he raised his hand. Delighted that Norm had something to say, John called on him right away. "If you're going to get ice cream," Norm said, "go for the good stuff." From that day on, Norm talked and participated.

His sudden expression of his desires was sometimes dangerous. One day, when John and two other therapists were busy helping other students, Norm got up and walked straight out of the classroom. No one had noticed, and when I called it to their attention, several therapists went flying out the door to catch him. Thank goodness the yard was fenced, so he couldn't wander into the street. In fact, he was trying to figure a way over the fence and onto the campus when they reached him and led him back. He didn't resist, and the three of them entered the classroom as if nothing had happened. Norm sat in his chair for the rest of the session, but this was the first time he had expressed through his actions that he did not want to be in TLC.

Golf and Bowling

Norm quickly learned exhibiting good behavior would earn him a voucher for points, and if he saved his points, he could trade them for a Snickers candy bar, his favorite. I don't think he really understood the meaning of the exchange, but he really like the idea of getting a Snickers, so the system motivated him to do whatever was necessary to get the reward.

Around this time, I asked Grace, Norm's occupational therapist, if Norm could go to the local golf driving range to see what would happen. She agreed to take Norm and a few other Casa Colina residents. I arranged for a golf pro to work with Norm. Grace was eager to provide the special help we needed. I arrived at TLC with Norm's golf clubs strapped on my shoulder. Norm recognized the clubs, but wasn't excited with the basic instructions from the pro, even though he was able to hit the ball on his first try, driving it about 150 yards. Instead of feeling happy that he could hit the ball, Norm was upset that its path wasn't straight. Grace was surprised and enthusiastic, saying that Norm had a natural golf swing. Despite Norm's frustration, seeing him engaging in activities he had always enjoyed was encouraging. As so often happened on our journey out of the darkness, the smallest ray of light helped us continue on the path.

Our next excursion with TLC was to the bowling alley. I was surprised that Norm wanted to go, because he'd always hated bowling, but it seemed that his short-term memory loss had allowed him to forget that. When we got there, I noticed several adaptive devices. a raised chute had been placed on the alley, allowing easy placement of the ball, which would roll down the chute and hit the pins. Quite a few Casa Colina residents couldn't roll the ball themselves, but each week they got together to bowl, anyway. When the therapist asked for a volunteer, Norm looked enthusiastic — until he sent the first ball down the alley. He suddenly remembered how much he hated bowling, and he never went back. To this day, he laughs when I remind him of the look on his face when the ball left his hand and went careening down the alley, just as his memory returned for a moment.

Fortunately, Norm was a pleasant person to be around, which wasn't the case with all brain-injured people. The staff liked Norm a lot, which was a nice surprise for them. Before he arrived, when they learned that he was a commander in the navy and a VP in his job, they were afraid he'd be hard to handle, but he quickly won their admiration and affection. As time passed and he learned to communicate, everything got easier.

When Norm first arrived at TLC, his inability to speak was a tremendous source of frustration. As time went on and he began to communicate, he was able to let me know that the staff had talked down to him and had raised their voices almost to a yell — not to upset him, but to make sure he understood. Now that he could answer questions and tell them what he needed, they were beginning to treat him more respectfully. I was pleased that they were talking nicely to him now, but even happier that Norm could finally tell the difference.

Each of his activities was moving along at a different pace and rhythm. For example, he couldn't differentiate between paper money and coins, and following directions was almost impossible. His balance was good. He could walk for twenty minutes, and do another twenty on the stationary bike when he got used to it, but each time he tried something new, it was like starting all over again. I watched the dedicated staff members teach Norm to take a deep breath, relax, and slow down when he got frustrated. I saw them teach him to read a few words, like his name. But he couldn't remember the staff's names, and objects were confusing to him, both in recognizing and naming them. In fact, his memory was so severely impaired that he couldn't remember the present moment a minute after it was over, and he couldn't store or retrieve new memories.

Life was a bumpy ride as I cheered my husband's small victories and grieved his failures and frustrations along with him. I don't know how I would have survived without the good wishes from our closest friends. I hung their cards along a string pinned to the wall in Norm's room, hoping they would mean something to him. He looked at me like a puppy, unable to understand when I pulled down one of the cards from a special friend, Lance, to read aloud. On the front was a picture of Winnie the Pooh standing next to Piglet. The caption read, "It is hard to be brave," said Piglet, "when you are only a Very Small Animal." Inside was written, "But sometimes it's easier to be brave with two. I hope you know how much I care."

I wiped a tear from my eye as I returned the card to the string. I hoped Lance knew how important he was to us as Norm was beginning life anew in his fifties — and so was I.

Chapter Eight

Homeward Bound

The First Visit

Norm wanted to come home. I guess he felt that two weeks in residence at TLC was enough, and every day, the first thing he did after he hugged me was ask me when he was going home. I avoided answering, thinking at first that his loss of short-term memory would cause him to forget. Well, he may have forgotten how to brush his teeth, but he remembered how much he wanted to leave Casa Colina. Each morning, he'd ask what I'd done about getting him discharged. I kept distracting him, but he didn't forget.

I couldn't understand what made Norm choose a certain subject to pursue relentlessly. I suspected it was a throwback to his former personality before the brain injury, when he was a driven, highly successful businessman. My frustration was that while he had grabbed hold of his need to be home, he'd forgotten the skills that would allow him to achieve his goal.

I spoke with Norm's therapists and caseworkers about his burning desire to leave. They felt he wasn't ready. So did I. All of us agreed that bringing Norm home at that point would be a big mistake. Norm disagreed with all of us, becoming quite vocal about going, grilling me as to whom I was consulting and advising me to go over their heads to their bosses. His previous unwillingness to take no for an answer was re-emerging from beneath his cloud of confusion, and he wouldn't drop it. I drove home each night asking myself the same question: How could he forget what I told him five minutes ago, yet remember with unwavering intent that he wants to come home? I suppose that same intent is how Norm recovered so dramatically, but at the time, it was problematic for both of us.

One day, Norm told me that if I continued to do nothing he would sign himself out. I didn't bother asking how he knew he couldn't be held against his will. He must have been talking with other residents and someone told him, but he didn't remember who had filled his head with this information. He knew only what he wanted and when he wanted it. Every incident that occurred during this crucial phase in his recovery confirmed how hard it was to fully understand how much the injury had impacted him. I was beginning to see that each person is a unique case requiring trial and error. I explained to Norm that we would both benefit greatly from his staying in residence for a few months.

In the end, his unrelenting attitude earned him a home visit, with his caseworker, Jane, by his side the whole time. Since Norm wouldn't back down, the staff made the decision, albeit against their better judgment. *The stubborn part of him hasn't changed a bit,* I thought, as I waited at home for Norm and Jane to arrive. This would be his first visit since his life had changed.

I had shown him photographs of our house to orient him before his arrival, but none of them had looked familiar to him — until they got off the freeway. Jane later told me that while Norm was enjoying the view, he was showing her the streets she had to take to get him home. He was right, and continued to direct the van until they pulled up to the front door. I met them outside to watch Norm walk across the entryway to the house. He passed straight through the atrium and the glass doors that led into the living room. He might have been unable to make the connection through pictures, but now that he was home, he knew just where everything was.

Jane had gone inside first to check for potential safety hazards, such as loose rugs, stairs, or railings. Luckily, we have a one-story home with no stairs to negotiate. A few steps behind Jane, Norm and I walked into the living room and out onto the deck. He looked as if he were reliving a dream as he scanned the table and chairs and admired the flowers. "I like it here," he finally said, "and I want to come home and stay."

After an hour, when Jane said they needed to beat the traffic back to Casa Colina, I was surprised that Norm didn't resist. It broke my heart to see him on his best behavior so he'd be allowed back to his own house. He didn't seem at all interested in his personal things; rather, he liked the overall feel of his own home. Jane and I agreed that the visit had gone much better than we expected, so we scheduled more weekend visits.

I knew it was only a matter of time before Norm came home for good. In a sense, he had gone on strike, sitting in the classrooms but doing no work. He was so unhappy that I wondered if he might get better faster if he could live at home. After all, he was sleeping through the night now, and performing most personal tasks, like dressing himself and eating, alone.

I looked into the outpatient program, which would require my driving him back and forth each day. I was already going to Casa Colina every day, so that wouldn't change, but what about the few spare moments away from Norm, when I paid bills, made appointments, and straightened up the house? What about getting the car serviced, or my personal maintenance, such as doctor's appointments and getting my hair done? How would I find the time? I already had no life of my own with Norm as a Casa Colina resident, and knew it would only get worse when he was discharged.

I'll figure all that out as I go along, I told myself, and made arrangements for Norm to become an outpatient. He was just so unhappy, and my gut told me he would figure out a way to get out of there on his own. I might as well accept the inevitable and participate in his discharge, even though his three-month stay would be drastically shortened.

On a Friday night, three weeks after he checked in, I packed up Norm's personal things, said goodbye to the staff, and got into the car. Norm didn't participate in any of the departure activities, and didn't appear disturbed or confused. He was going home.

Norm's Closet

Once I'd gotten Norm unpacked, he wandered through the house, exploring everything. He walked into his closet and stared at his clothing, pulling plastic laundry coverings off his suits and shirts to see what was there. He spent hours sorting his shirts, pants, and jackets, as if trying to figure out who he used to be. He held up a bright pink golf shirt and said to me, "This must belong to someone else. I would never wear it."

When he opened the door to another walk-in closet, he jumped back. All his shoes had been lying there in no particular order since before his accident. He hadn't cared then, but life was different now. "No brain-injured person should own so many pairs of shoes that look so alike," he admonished me. With a pang of guilt, I shut the door, vowing to create a system for him so he could easily pick out a matching pair of shoes.

I looked around and found an empty wine rack, then I guided Norm back to the closet and showed him how to put one shoe in each space. He smiled, feeling in control of the situation now, since there weren't so many scattered shoes to consider. When I told him which shoes were for playing tennis and walking, and which were for casual wear and dress, he asked why so many of them looked the same. I explained that people who like certain styles often bought them in black and brown. But why were certain pairs called "tennis shoes," he asked, if he didn't wear them to play tennis? And how did I clean them? I explained that some had to be polished, and others could be thrown into the washing machine, depending on whether they were leather or canvas.

Over the next weeks, Norm spent a lot of time in his closet, trying to determine his personality from his clothing. I separated everything into categories: casual, dress, golf, and tennis. Once he could recognize the categories, he could pick out what he wanted to wear for any event or purpose. I'd never thought about these simple, everyday decisions we make, until I saw the difficulties that arose when such things didn't come naturally.

There was just so much for Norm to consider, like the fit of his clothing now that he was gaining back his weight. And there were the weather changes: it was starting to get warmer and rain was in the forecast. I told Norm he had to observe the weather before he got dressed, choosing lighter clothing for warm weather and heavier for cold — if he could tell the difference. It seemed as though each time I'd tell him to dress light, it would cool down and rain. Finally, I told him to walk naked into our enclosed atrium, see whether he felt warm or cold, and dress accordingly.

Brainpower

While Norm was learning about his clothing and how to dress himself, we also had to concentrate on other skills that would permit him an independent life. Thank goodness Norm liked going to Casa Colina, now that he didn't have to live there, because we attended classes or outings each day as part of TLC. We headed home every evening at 4:30 or 5, which allowed little time for grocery shopping or anything else. We ended up eating all of our meals out, since I had to watch over Norm at every moment. I couldn't leave him alone in the car or at home, leaving no opportunity to shop, cook, and prepare meals. I hated that, but what could I do?

Even the weekends were full, as I drove Norm along the various freeways he had driven hundreds of times before, explaining the numbers, billboards, and makes and models of the other cars — anything to keep his mind active, which is the foundation for all ABI therapy. For example, at Casa Colina, they would take Norm and the other students on safety walks, where they relearned signals, and the meaning of crosswalks and pedestrian right of way. Six graduates from TLC had been struck by cars and died the previous year, so this was the first time that safety walks were part of the curriculum.

Deeply grateful for any help along the way, I was thrilled when Keith, one of Norm's business associates, became involved in his recovery. Keith would come to the house to remind Norm of people he used to know. He even devised an organizational chart of Norm's employees, putting their names next to their positions, with a photo glued on so Norm could learn to recognize them. Incidentally, Keith quit his job later that year, because it wasn't as satisfying for him without Norm as his manager. Without people like Keith, who constantly reminded me about "the silver lining" in any situation, I don't know what I would have done.

Even with Keith's help and that of other well-meaning people, it was a tough time. While Norm was working to increase his brainpower, I was getting him dressed each day, attending doctor's appointments and meetings with the staff, and sitting beside Norm each day, learning to teach him what he needed to get back into the world. He slowly picked up his name, address, and phone number, and was soon remembering his birthday, where he was born, and the names of his children. He had forgotten most everything, but it gave me hope to see him begin picking up a few things here and there.

I learned a great deal about brain injury during that time, while feeling like I was chasing my tail around just to get through a day. Norm was still in therapy with John, and, now that the weather was nice, we all sat in the garden under the umbrella, working with Norm to get his life back.

I knew little about his condition other than that Norm was diagnosed with anoxia, a condition caused by oxygen deprivation, which severely impairs the memory's storage and retrieval systems. As a result, Norm's problem-solving neurons were damaged and objects were confusing to him. Anoxia also had damaged the executive portion of his brain, impacting his visual perception, his attention span, and his ability to sit still and concentrate. Additionally, he was diagnosed with aphasia, which caused his inability to find words and name things.

I studied relentlessly, finding out that the brain is constantly making neurological connections, relaying information from one nerve cell to the next. The relearning stage is all about repetition, similar to when things were learned for the first time. You see, when certain neurons (electrical impulses that act as individual processing systems) are damaged, they will never heal. You never lose learned information. Just the connection to it. Which is like the bridge is blown up and you have to construct a new bridge. The more you knew before the brain injury, the better chance of your recovery.

The brain has to figure out how to send information to a healthy neuron instead of a dead one, which requires repeating things over and over. Eventually, the brain picks a healthy neuron to hold the new information, and begins to bypass the damaged ones. It can take a month or a year, even though it appears that a brain-injured person can suddenly remember things he or she forgot yesterday. With an enormous amount of tedious repetition, a person with ABI eventually gets it, as functions that were futile in damaged cells are transferred to healthy ones.

Even now, seven years later, Norm continues to heal, though it is less evident and dramatic than in the beginning. His continuous recovery over the years validates my original decision to take him to TLC to improve his life. What if I had considered my husband brain dead and done nothing to further his education, as so many caregivers end up doing? I would have lost my husband again and again, instead of seeing him grow and learn, and celebrating his triumphs.

It was far from easy, but Norm and I are proof that with the right amount of faith, will, and concentration, a lot of healing can happen.

Chapter Nine

Double Trouble

An Early Release

Having just brought Norm home after a long day at school, I walked over to the fax machine as a matter of routine, but when I read the piece of paper in my hands, routine was nowhere to be found. The startling message from Casa Colina began, "We were unable to reach you by telephone."

That made no sense. I was at Casa Colina every day. In fact, I'd just come from there and the management knew that. The fax continued, "We have been unable to get further insurance authorization for Norm's outpatient daycare. We recommend outpatient therapy three times a week at a different facility of your choice."

Stunned, I could barely finish reading the fax. It seemed that Norm's caseworker would mail us a prescription for speech therapy, along with the community college resource list. So that was the end? We were out, just like that? I became angry and terrified at the same time; they were releasing Norm without ever discussing it with me or giving any warning. Where was their humanity? Norm needed much more help, and I had no idea where to get it. He was in no condition to attend college classes. He didn't know how to read, write, drive a car, add numbers, write a check, or handle money. "How could they do this?" I repeated, as a mantra, over and over.

At the same time, Norm's cardiologist was concerned about Norm's heart. Ever since the accident, the doctor had wanted to implant a defibrillator in Norm's chest, but, given his mental state, they thought it was too dangerous for him to undergo surgery; the doctor felt that just lying on the table would be impossible at this time. They agreed to continue his medications until his mental capacity improved. They warned us, however, that if he continued having sustained runs of what they called "ventricular tachycardia" (irregular heart activity), the doctor would have to implant a defibrillator under general anesthesia. At least by now, they expected Norm to live, a far cry from his coma days, when life or death was in question.

At the end of February 1997, just days before Casa Colina was throwing us out, Norm was scheduled for an angiogram, to determine the condition of his arteries. The doctor asked me to be in the operating room while they performed it. Norm was unaware of what was happening, so they wanted me on hand in case they needed to communicate something that only I could make him understand. Frank was there, too, refusing when they asked him to wait outside. It turned out to be important that he was there: the combination of Frank's and my presence made Norm feel safe enough to get on the table and stay there.

In a few moments, two blockages were found. One could be cleared immediately with an angioplasty, a procedure that clears the arteries with a balloon-like instrument that enlarges them and removes blockages. Once that was done, a permanent stent, a small cylinder of wire mesh, was inserted to hold the artery open. The second area was too hidden to reach, since the available stents were not flexible enough for that particular blockage. Apparently, there was a stent that would work, but the FDA hadn't yet approved it, so Norm was scheduled for another surgery to receive an Implantable Cardioverter Defibrillator (ICD).

Here I was, having to make a decision to have a device I knew nothing about implanted in my husband's body. I hated the responsibility, but had no choice. I wanted Norm to live; we'd come this far, and there was no turning back.

ICD, Our New Friend

While busy fighting Casa Colina and trying to figure out where to send Norm next, I hurried to an appointment to find out what an ICD was and how it worked. The doctor, a respected thoracic and cardiovascular surgeon, had been referred by Norm's internist. I remember being so tired that the thought of taking on one more thing was overwhelming, but there was no one else to do the job.

In the waiting room, I filled out the appropriate forms, working hard to stay awake until my name was called. When I entered the inner office, I met the surgeon, who wore scrubs, and a gentleman dressed in a business suit. He was a representative from Medtronic, the company that manufactured the ICD. I was reassured by his presence, knowing he could answer any questions I might have. He showed me how the original ICD had looked, then they showed me the new, improved version. Medtronic had made major strides in reducing the size of their ICD, which eliminated cutting the chest open and breaking ribs to implant it, as they had before.

I thought back wistfully to February 1991, when Norm had collapsed at the airport. The defibrillator should have been put in place back then, which could have spared Norm his brain injury and all that was to follow. Tears formed, but I forced them back. *What's done is done,* I thought, as I studied the device that was about to be put in my husband's chest. The new ICD was about the size of a small bar of soap. The surgeon explained that he would make an incision in Norm's left shoulder to implant it.

I listened carefully, having no idea what questions to ask, or whether the procedure was safe, or if this doctor was the right one to perform it. He explained that the device had a thin insulated wire (a lead) with electrodes (electrical contacts) located near the tip. It was threaded through a vein and secured to the inside of the heart. If the heart pumped the blood too quickly, which would cause a heart attack, the ICD would be activated with an electric shock that would slow the heart enough to allow the proper amount of blood to flow through. After all of ten minutes for the entire meeting, I was sent home with a dozen brochures to read, so I could educate myself — after we made the surgery appointment.

Between our impending exit from Casa Colina and facing Norm's surgery, no amount of self-talk could get me to sleep. Each time I started to drop off, I would jerk awake, feeling abandoned and betrayed, with no idea what to do. Where would I start? What kind of therapy did Norm need? Where would we go next? Was I making the right decisions for him?

When it was finally light enough to call TLC about the fax, they acted distant, citing Norm's upcoming surgery and his expected recovery time as a reason to end his work with them. His lessons would be interrupted, and besides, they felt they had given him everything they could. Why didn't I call some local hospitals to find out what they offered?

I hung up in a rage. Did they think I was looking for someone to give my husband a flu shot? This was serious. Norm needed continued schooling, and they were obviously prepared to do nothing. I was in a state of shock at first, and desperate, but had to pull out of it right away. Thank God I'd sat in on all of Norm's classes and knew what they had taught him; I could use the knowledge to create an appropriate program that would give Norm back his skills.

For lack of anything better to do, I listed the things I wanted Norm to re-learn: the use of his computer and calculator, and how to read the newspaper. But when I took the list to a local hospital, they told me they didn't do that kind of therapy, and were unwilling to experiment with a new method. I trudged from facility to facility with no success — until I arrived at Glendale Adventist Medical Center.

The director of rehabilitation there was interested in my program and wanted to show it to Teresa, one of their speech and language pathologists. May God bless Teresa, who thought my suggested curriculum reasonable. When she agreed to it, I was relieved that I wouldn't have to become Norm's primary tutor on top of everything else. For now, I could concentrate on the surgery. If only I'd known about Good Samaritan Hospital's ICD support group of about 200 people, run by an internationally known cardiologist, Doctor David Cannom, of whom I could have asked my defibrillator questions. But I had no resources or information back then.

The Implant

The surgery was over in a short time, and there were no complications. When they wheeled Norm out of the OR, he had a defibrillator under his left pectoral muscle, and the five-inch incision on his shoulder was neatly stitched. Apparently, that area of implantation was the best choice, though it had made the surgery slightly more complicated. The biggest win was that pectoral placement of the device made it more stable, and it was invisible when Norm wasn't wearing a shirt. Improving his quality of life was the most important consideration.

Norm recovered by the next day, but it was another month before he could understand what had happened to him. I was relieved he'd made it through yet another procedure, even though I couldn't explain it to him — I barely understood it myself. I knew only that the defibrillator was in place, prepared to shock his heart if needed, which would be tough on both of us. I fantasized what would happen if it went off while we were asleep. How would Norm react to the shock? Would he understand enough for me to help him? I prayed it would never happen, even though I knew it was crucial to his life.

Ignorant and frightened, I completed a CPR class, hoping it would help in case the defibrillator shocked Norm. With so many questions and fears, I scheduled us for several sessions with a trauma therapist. It was a good idea, but while the woman knew a lot about the effects of bank robberies, car accidents, and plane crashes, she had never worked with a person with a brain injury or an ICD. The only useful suggestion she gave us was to have the manufacturer give us a full explanation of the engineering and function of the ICD.

I made the appointment with Medtronic. On arriving there, the first thing we did was to spend an hour and a half touching the paraphernalia that accompanied the device and asking questions:

Q: What is the ICD made from?
A: Titanium.
Q: How long will the battery last?
A: Four to six years, meaning that Norm would have to undergo a surgical procedure every four or five years, to replace the old one with a new one.
Q: How does the tubing fit into the heart?
A: It's threaded through a vein and into the heart.
Q: Will I get shocked if I touch Norm while he's being shocked?
A: You might feel it, but it would be minimal.

I got the answers, but even if I hadn't, we had to accept the ICD; if we remained at odds with it, we'd never learn to understand or appreciate it. And when Norm smiled broadly and declared himself a bionic man, that was good enough for me. We left the doctor's office with brochures and information that I wished I'd gotten before the surgery, but the old cliché "Better late than never" would have to apply because there was a new challenge to face. Now that the surgery to keep Norm alive was done, I needed to help make his life worthwhile, by working with the therapist at Glendale Adventist Medical Center to improve Norm's most basic skills.

Living with the ICD has become easier with each passing day. It allows us a fairly normal life; we can travel and engage in exercise and sports. We both carry cards with pictures of the device and where it's implanted, especially if we go to a country where little English is spoken. Via the Internet, I have access to a list of doctors and hospitals that work with ICDs, so we feel pretty secure about it.

To this day, the doctor reads out the ICD every three months by placing a hand-held magnet over it. The ICD information is printed in a way that resembles an EKG report. I'm happy to say that the device has so far not had to give Norm a shock. We know it might be traumatic if it ever does, but we'll welcome it, because it will also be saving his life.

Chapter Ten

Back in the Saddle

The Monster Bike

N orm recovered from his implant in record time, but he fell into a depression that lasted for several months. All he wanted to do was sit in front of the television and watch whatever was on. Nothing I said changed his mind. He seemed content to sit perfectly still for hours, staring at the screen, watching soap operas and game shows — no more PBS, CNN, or History Channel.

I never found out what drew him to these mindless shows; I knew only that he'd lost his connection to almost everything. Maybe he was trying to regain a sense of reality, but soap operas were hardly the way to do it. I lost patience with his physical stagnation when I walked into the living room one afternoon and found him just where he'd been since breakfast. I think it was the blank expression on his face that made me raise my voice and say, "What is it going to take to get you away from the TV and start getting active?"

"I want to ride my bicycle," he answered quickly. My mind shot back to the day of his accident. I pictured his racing bike on its side, wheels spinning in the air while he lay on the highway, bleeding, dying. I heard the whine of the ambulance rushing him to the emergency room. All that was what his bike had come to represent to me, and I wasn't sure I wanted to test my own mettle by getting him back on it again. Was I ready for this? More important, was he?

His racing bike had been hanging in the garage since the day I'd brought it back from San Diego. It was built for speed, not durability, and I was surprised that it had needed only fifty dollars' worth of adjustments after the accident. Considering fifty dollars against the $500,000 that Norm's brain damage had cost so far, the bike was cheap in comparison. I bought Norm a mountain bike, however, anticipating his desire to ride again; if and when it happened, I was determined that he'd never get back on the racing bike. The mountain bike was safer and stronger, even if it didn't look as spiffy.

I'd seen Norm standing in the garage, staring at his bike from time to time since he'd gotten home, but neither of us had spoken about it — until today. I frowned at both of the unwelcome guests hanging in the garage. *Better get over it,* I thought, pulling down the mountain bike. I pumped up the tires and wheeled it out front, engaging in a monologue of grumbling and praying mixed together. Once again, I had to let go and make sure nothing stopped Norm from moving forward — including me.

I lifted the two-wheeled monster into the rack on the back of our truck, put mine beside it, got Norm in the passenger seat, and off we went. Before his heart attack, Norm and I often exercised by riding our bikes around the Rose Bowl. That was where we were headed now, but not to the stadium itself; I wanted to take Norm to the parking lot for a practice run first, so we could determine which skills he'd lost and which he'd retained. I couldn't allow him to fall off a moving bike and get injured again.

We sped along the 210 freeway, turning off at the Rose Bowl exit. I yearned for last year, when we'd done this together with no cares at all. Turning right and heading downhill toward the Rose Bowl, I looked ahead at the soft green grass on the adjoining golf course. We had golfed there many times before the accident, and I'd have given anything to be able to turn back time.

There was no event at the Rose Bowl that day, and the enormous parking lot was empty. We had it all to ourselves, just as I'd planned. I parked in the center, where Norm would have lots of room to maneuver. He was so excited, he literally bounced out of the truck. He was smiling for the first time in months as he helped me remove the bungee cords holding our bikes. Norm's enthusiasm helped me overcome my fear as I grabbed our gloves, helmets, and water bottles. I couldn't stop thinking about the blood-soaked bike clothing they'd had to cut off of Norm when he was in a coma.

At least he had a good helmet, which offered me a little security. When we first bought our bikes, Norm had insisted we invest in the best helmets available, not knowing that his insistence would someday save his life. He'd been wearing the helmet, thank God, when he fell after his heart attack, and though it was covered in blood and cracked on the left side, it had kept his head in one piece. Norm's brain damage resulted from the lack of oxygen, not the fall itself, and it would have been worse if he hadn't been wearing his helmet. We'd sent it back to the manufacturer, who had replaced it at no cost. Now, I made sure it was snugly placed on Norm's head, and buckled tightly.

Once we'd put on the rest of our gear, I balanced my bike on its kickstand and went to assist Norm. He was having a hard time getting his foot over the center bar, so I showed him how to lean the bike downward to accommodate his mount and dismount. He shot me a strange look, obviously feeling unnatural, but he persevered — like a determined kid learning to ride for the first time.

I stabilized Norm's bike by standing in front of him and placing the wheel between my legs while he got on the saddle. He sat there, looking unsure. I wanted him to get the feeling of sitting on the bike and how to work the chrome-handled brakes attached to each side of the handlebars. I lowered his seat enough to make sure he could put his feet down and scrape the pavement without having to stretch, in case of the need for a sudden stop.

Once I saw that Norm's balance seemed fine and he had no trouble with the brakes or the gears, it was time to see what he could do. My heart raced as I remembered the First-Aid kit in the truck. If anything happened, I would become Nurse Dora. Norm, of course, had no idea what he was capable of, so we had no choice but to give it the old navy try.

Norm suddenly shot forward, so I hopped on my bike and pedaled fast to catch up with him. He seemed to be doing well, and he was smiling from ear to ear. We circled the huge parking lot several times before I asked if he was ready to rest. I really didn't want him to stop, fearing that he might forget to slow down or to put one foot on the concrete before he got off. It was a lot for him to remember, but we couldn't keep riding around the parking lot until the sun went down.

I thanked God when Norm remembered to slow down and apply the brake without throwing himself over the handlebars. He did have a little trouble figuring out how to stop the bike and balance it at the same time, though, scraping the sole off one of his tennis shoes. But he didn't care and neither did I — he had ridden, and he was alive and well.

When we got back on terra firma, Norm had a look of success on his face that I hadn't seen since before his brain injury. It was the glow of self-esteem, and from then on, it grew each time he did something new. The better his self-esteem, the more confident he became at trying new things. He got back in the truck tired but happy, insisting that we celebrate his latest victory with a pit stop at Starbucks. A Cappuccino Grande never tasted so good!

We sat outside in the sun, an umbrella shading our faces, while Norm stared at his new Timex watch, wanting to know if it was time for lunch. He had a hard time remembering the date and the day of the week, so having them on his watch was a plus. It had taken awhile to figure out what kind of watch would meet all of Norm's needs, but it obviously needed a large face with a white background, and no Roman numerals or dots on the quarter-hour.

We finished our coffee, stopped at Trader Joe's, picked up salads to go, and headed home.

Repetition and More Spills

Once we were back home, I knew what Norm needed most: I showed him how to mount and dismount the stationary bike I'd set up in the back room. It was back to the relearning stage, the endless repetitions. I decided to break the routine into small individual actions, which I had Norm practice for the next month. Grab the handlebars, balance, tilt the bike downward, put one leg over the bar, sit on the saddle… over and over and over.

We continued to ride at the Rose Bowl, and, eventually, at a local park three miles from home. The idea was to give Norm practice in a more confined area, since the park's lot was small and a good number of people were walking around in it. I wanted him to be aware of them, but to stay focused on the task at hand and not become distracted.

When he was doing better, Norm and I went up to Big Bear Lake to practice riding with Frank. This would be the first time we took a bike ride on the road, and I needed to check Norm's alertness. I was relieved when we pulled up to my son's cottage. I was getting some help, which was a welcome change.

We ate lunch outside on the wooden table and chairs that Frank had painted in bright colors. Immediately following lunch, Norm was anxious to get going. We were a determined threesome as we got on our bikes in the front yard and took off down the driveway. Norm rode just behind Frank, and I took up the rear, watching at each intersection to see if Norm was anticipating cars. He exhibited no problems with judgment or awareness of other vehicles, so we rode on for a couple of miles, making a stop to visit at a friend's house. When we got back on the road and headed home, we were all feeling great about how well Norm was doing.

He was so relaxed on the bike, in fact, that I smiled when he passed both Frank and me in the last few yards leading into the driveway. But the next thing I knew, Norm had run straight into Frank's boat and trailer, which were parked in the driveway. By the time we were running toward him, he was dragging both feet on the ground trying to stop. "I'm having a heart attack!" he yelled — my worst fear realized.

Arriving at the place in the dirt where Norm had fallen, I quickly evaluated that he was not having a heart attack. Rather, he'd had the wind knocked out of him when he hit his chest, and had mistaken the pressure he'd felt when he tried to get to his feet. Frank and I were both so upset that we started yelling at each other while I tried to get Norm standing. He didn't want my help, and, thankfully, Frank took control, telling us both to be quiet while he assessed Norm's injuries. I walked away, too upset to be any help to anyone.

With Frank's help, Norm was on his feet in about ten minutes, while I muttered to myself, wondering if I'd survive this ordeal. Norm had dirt all over his body, and some bloody cuts and bruises, but he was all right. I dressed his wounds, and soon enough we were all calm, sitting on the deck, sipping cold drinks. I shook my head and wondered what on earth had just happened. Did we have a success or a failure? There was no telling. All I was sure of was that Norm wanted to know when he could ride again.

More Spills

On another visit to Big Bear Lake, a young boy in our neighborhood wanted Norm to go riding with him. I was against it, but Norm wouldn't take no for an answer. He took off with the boy while I raided the refrigerator to calm my nerves. When I had finally talked myself down and was reading a book on the front porch, the boy came speeding to the house to tell us there had been an accident. Frank jumped into the car and quickly returned with Norm, who had taken a spill and hurt himself again. It was only cuts and bruises, but, after two accidents, it was clear that I needed to put Norm through some more intensive training.

His main problem wasn't with riding, it was with mounting and dismounting, slowing down, and applying the brakes. I was frustrated that the part of his brain that told him how to ride didn't tell him how to do the rest. Once again, it was repetition after repetition, retraining his brain to transmit messages to healthy neurons, just as we'd done all along. And just like before, I had no idea whether it would take two days, two weeks, or two years. However long, it was back to the stationary bike, where I broke down the mount and dismount into individual steps, encouraging Norm to practice them again and again until the actions became automatic.

Then we went to Venice Beach, where I rented us a couple of three-wheelers, hoping to restore Norm's sense of balance and keep him safe at the same time. It helped, and I was able to teach him to listen to what was behind him and recognize the sounds of another bike, a car, or a roller skater, so he could slow down and let them pass.

To this day, he continues to ride his mountain bike with great pleasure. I'm always a little nervous about it, but I'm grateful that, so far, he hasn't asked to ride the racing bike. I know he will someday, and it'll be important that he get back on the bike that threw him. But for now, he's content to stare at it in the garage, and I'm content to silently wonder what he's thinking.

Chapter Eleven

Finding His Way

The Third Grade

Now that Norm had a pair of wheels beneath him, it was time to get some real answers as to how much his data bank of knowledge had deteriorated. So, in April 1997, Norman Camp, oceanographer and Ph.D., tested below the third-grade level. Reality hit home once again, while Teresa, one of Norm's new speech pathologists, set up a program with goals attainable by a struggling third grader. Trying not to get discouraged, I concentrated on finding a way for Norm to get back and forth from Glendale Adventist Medical Center three times a week.

I couldn't do it all myself, so I took a doctor's note, verifying Norm's brain injury, to a transportation company. They agreed to pick Norm up at home three days a week, deliver him to the Medical Center, and drive him home in the late afternoon. Often, however, that company wouldn't show up in the morning, so I'd throw on something at the last moment and take him myself. Or, I might receive a call from the Medical Center late in the day, telling me that Norm was standing in the lobby. This was taking up too much energy, so I eventually canceled the transportation service and did the driving myself. It was yet another supposed community service that caused more angst than peace of mind, and we were paying for it with our tax dollars! I wished these programs would work with us instead of against us, but soon stopped thinking about it. I simply couldn't allow anything to get in the way of my primary goal: getting Norm whatever he needed to improve his quality of life.

I proceeded according to a plan, making sure Norm did his homework assignments each night: reading the newspaper headlines, writing the alphabet, learning to recognize money, and keeping a journal of that day's activities. One of the challenges was that Norm went to school each day, so we couldn't start his homework until the late afternoon or early evening — the worst time for someone with a brain injury. I was quickly learning that a person with ABI expends ten times as much energy as a healthy person would to do the same things, especially at the end of a long, tiring day. Still, nothing would deter us from our goal.

During this time, the president of Norm's company was holding open Norm's vice-presidential position for a year, in case he could return to work. As kind as this was, it put a lot of pressure on both of us, because no one at work really understood Norm's diminished abilities. He looked fine, just like the old Norm, since all of his cuts and bruises healed. But he had a long way to go.

The medical center staff was very helpful, agreeing to work with me on a strategy to help Norm attend a meeting with his business cronies. The company president had scheduled the meeting in San Diego, with all the various divisions in attendance. If Norm went, it would be the first time his associates had seen him since his heart attack. At first he didn't want to go; I didn't push, because I'd have hated to see him embarrassed, and he felt the same way. After some discussion, however, Norm decided to attend the meeting after all. He hadn't seen his work group for some time, and was anxious to find out how things were going.

Getting him there wasn't my biggest concern; I told Norm I'd make sure he arrived on time. But what if he had to use the facilities and there was no one to help him? I imagined him walking around the building, searching for the men's room and having no idea how to get back to the conference room. Gwen, another of his speech pathologists, and Teresa began taking him to the lobby and cafeteria of the Medical Center, giving him clues for finding his way back. They helped him notice names, numbers, and directional arrows along the way, with the promise of a Snickers motivating him to remember the location of the gift shop.

This phase of Norm's recovery was exceptionally difficult; it was important that I, the caregiver, work closely with the therapists, following their advice and direction. I didn't want to get in the way of Norm's recovery, so I had to let go of my protector role and let him start demonstrating some independence. At the end of two weeks, Norm was successfully maneuvering his way around the medical center — and eating too many Snickers bars!

The day we checked into the hotel in San Diego, I wondered what I was getting us into. The next morning, when we stood at the elevator and I noticed Norm had on one black shoe and one brown, I further questioned the wisdom of this meeting. Oh well, it was too late to go home, I thought, as we returned to the room to change Norm's shoes. He seemed unaffected by the incident, which reminded me to relax. Things weren't perfect, they never would be, and we had to accept things as they were if Norm were to make successful changes.

Norm settled into the front row of the conference room, next to the company president. Norm felt a little bit like one of the guys, but he didn't interact much, because he was still having trouble finding the right words to say and didn't want to embarrass himself. The good news was that he recognized everyone. That was surprising, because he was having a hard time with his memory, but he made it through the entire meeting without any embarrassing incidents. The success felt great to both of us.

Progress

Another way that Norm made progress was by bringing his laptop computer to his therapy sessions. He kept a journal of each day's events as he relearned his computer skills. Since the heart attack, he could only read white lettering on a black background, but when Teresa cut a rectangular section out of a piece of paper, and put it over each word to isolate it, Norm started reading words. In a while, he was able to read black lettering on white as well, broadening the material available to him.

I was fascinated at Teresa's and Gwen's ability to create a method for whatever function we wanted Norm to learn. We were still eating our meals out, and when we returned from a different restaurant each day, they were eager to find out from Norm what he had eaten and how he had liked the food. One day, they asked him to draw a picture of the inside of the restaurant, and they all talked about it.

They also used his past work as an oceanographer to remind him about calculators. He had used a reverse polar calculator in advanced work, and soon after he began relearning the calculator, he was teaching them. Similarly, when I bought him a Franklin Spell Check with a thesaurus, to look

up the spelling and meanings of words, he was slow at first, but eventually he got it.

"Slow" is a word I took seriously only after Norm's ABI. In this fast-
paced world, you see, it's nearly impossible for a person with a brain injury
to keep up. Simple things like telephone voice prompts move too fast, so
imagine the challenges connected with daily calls to pay bills, request information, register for school, or check out what's playing at the movies. Even
the speed at which people spoke was challenging. I told Norm to explain to
people that he couldn't process information when they talked too fast. He
used the analogy of a computer, telling them that his processor wouldn't
accept input at their speed. Thus, while Norm learned to take care of himself, he was also educating others about brain injury.

Back at home, I converted our dining room into a classroom with a white
board, flash cards for math, the kind of writing paper we used in first grade,
spelling books, games, puzzles, a small recorder for memory checks, calculators, and a laptop computer. Geared to supply teachers, a Young Scholar
store in Glendale helped me with a large selection of books and games.

I started Norm as in grammar school, printing a large "A" and small "a"
and continuing through the alphabet. His goal was to sign his name; we
were largely unsuccessful, until one night when a group of his male friends
took him to dinner. When Norm insisted on paying, but admitted that he
didn't know how to sign his name, the guys convinced him that nobody
cared how it looked. He scribbled his name and that was the beginning of
the return of his signature. His signature today is just as sloppy and illeg-
ible as it was twenty years ago, confirming that he's still a doctor — some
things never change.

Then there was money, which suddenly had no meaning whatsoever
for Norm. I bought a toy cash register and we started to learn the various
bills and coins and their value. There were some good money exercises in
the books I'd bought, but I thought it was important to use real money so
he could recognize it. This was one of the challenges we faced with ABI:
meanings and recognition of things often didn't translate from one object
to the next.

Getting pretty good at being adaptable, my plan was to cut the price tags
off newly bought items and pretend that Norm was buying them from me.
He would pay, I'd give him change, and then we'd start all over again. I had

no idea where we'd end up; I knew only that both of us were going to give it all we had.

I had to get creative about our outings, too, like going to the Farmers Market. When there was a crowd, I feared that Norm would get lost, and I got exhausted keeping an eye on him at all times. One day, though, while walking through Sports Chalet, I spotted some people using walkie-talkies. *That'll work,* I thought.

I purchased two walkie-talkie devices, both locked into the same channel, placing one around Norm's neck and the other in my pocket. If he got lost, he could push the button, describe his surroundings, and, if he stayed where he was, I could find him. This took some of the pressure off, and I could enjoy our outings, even if I was on rescue duty. At least, I knew where he was.

The Fight Goes On

While Norm continued going to Glendale Adventist Medical Center for the next four months, I never stopped fighting to get all the insurance benefits he was entitled to. Refusing to take the word of the insurance person on the telephone, I requested periodic evaluations and the appropriate doctor's letters to prove that Norm was still making progress and needed additional therapy.

It was relentless, but I thought back to the time, a month after Norm's injury, when a psychologist and other hospital staff had given me only discouraging and hopeless information. Norm had proven them wrong, and was continuing to, as he struggled to concentrate during the intensive two-hour sessions. These drained him, but he never complained; he just continued his efforts. Soon, they introduced electronic devices that were helpful with math. They also helped him with reading, composing, typing, sentence structure, and spelling.

At Radio Shack I found a battery-operated gadget called "The Memory Voice." This simple, inexpensive device, which fits on Norm's key chain, allowed him to leave a short message about his location, room number, and where the car was parked. One of Norm's worst problems was forgetting to put his credit card back in his wallet. I wanted him to have that independence, but couldn't keep canceling the card every time he lost it. While relaxing with a magazine, I saw a picture of a "beeping wallet," which starts beeping when you remove the credit card and doesn't quit until you replace it. It was amazing that, just when I needed something, it somehow appeared.

Norm's math continued to improve: one day, when we passed a chalkboard, he stopped and began writing out a long equation. No one in our group knew advanced math, and it was obvious that we had to get someone with high-level skills to accommodate Norm. I called Glendale College and requested a tutor. A German exchange student answered our ad and we hired him. I handed him a load of brochures on ABI. With his newfound understanding of how to assess Norm's weak points and develop his math program, he tutored Norm for about two months, until Norm decided it was time to venture out on his own. To my surprise and the tutor's, Norm thanked him and told him he was great, but that it was time for him to move on by himself. Norm always seemed to know, and most of the time, I went along with his decisions.

Norm came home from Glendale Adventist Medical Center one day and announced that he was finished with therapy. I wasn't thrilled, but I wasn't surprised either, since this had become his pattern. I felt he still needed more help than I could give him, and had spent months battling the insurance company to secure funds for more therapy. None of this mattered to Norm. He felt they had done what they could for him and it was up to him to continue on his own. I questioned his decision, but couldn't change his mind. The next day, we went to the hospital to tell the therapists about his choice. They were shocked, of course, but after hearing Norm's explanation, they were in agreement and wished him the best.

Norm continues to use software programs to strengthen his algebra, trigonometry, geometry, statistics, and physics, but the basic skills of reading and comprehension continue to be a struggle. Before his heart attack, Norm would read two or three novels a week, and had built up quite a library. Since he'd sustained ABI, however, he hadn't been able to read at all. Wondering what to do, I realized that I'd never taken him to an optometrist — maybe his eyes had been affected.

The eye doctor we consulted in 1998 insisted that ABI hadn't affected Norm's vision. On a second visit with the same doctor, however, the doctor found weakened muscles in Norm's eyes. He prescribed new reading glasses. Norm already had bifocals, so getting him another pair of glasses seemed illogical, but I got them anyway. When there was no improvement, Norm stopped using the glasses. Still, I refused to stop looking for answers.

Chapter Twelve

Skiing, Anyone?

The Basics

The leaves were turning fire red and orange, the air was crisp, and the days were getting shorter when Norm began asking, "When can I go skiing?"

Here we go again, I thought. Norm's brain injury was only ten months old and he was still relearning his basic skills one baby step at a time. Did it make a difference that Norm had first hit the ski slopes when he was four years old? As an adult, he had become what was called a "black diamond" skier, so skilled that I could only dream of performing at his level. I was a "blue run" skier, enjoying the easier slopes, meeting new friends on the lifts, admiring the icicles hanging from the trees, the profound silence, the serenity of the birds, and the blanket of snow that blended everything into a glorious world of cool, white silk. Norm was an accomplished athlete, skiing all over the world, the picture of grace, speed, and advanced skill.

Now, the very idea of Norm getting back on the slopes was unthinkable. He didn't even know how to put on the boots that clicked into his skis, or what they were for, and he had trouble with balance. It was as if he were looking at his poles for the first time, and now, with his defibrillator, it all seemed so dangerous and impractical. Yet, I simply had to come to terms with the fact that while he was learning third-grade math, Norm wanted to ski!

He was doing relatively well these days, but the idea of his careening down the ski slopes with his compromised balance and deductive reasoning was more than I could bear. To appease him, I told him he'd be skiing again someday, hoping he'd forget about it. I should have known better; after all, he was already back on the bike. It was only a matter of time, I realized, as he asked again and again about getting back on the slopes. He wanted specifics: whom had I called about making the actual arrangements? Where would we go for the first run?

When this continued for weeks, I knew there was no way he'd let go of his dream. Getting him to understand the difference between a ski pole and his helmet seemed next to impossible. As it was, I was nursing him twenty-four hours a day just to get him through a normal day. How could I take on this added burden? I'd have to find a way, because Norm wouldn't let me forget. He was determined to ski, and it was my job to figure out how we could accomplish the task.

Back when Norm was a resident at Casa Colina, they had mentioned something about an outdoor sports program, but Norm had been so busy relearning how to walk, talk and eat, that skiing was the farthest thing from my mind then. Things had changed. With a sigh, I tried to erase the mental picture of Norm and me, rolling down the hill, falling over each other all the way down, wondering what would happen when we eventually hit the bottom. Then I phoned Katie Spark, director of the Outdoor Adventures Program at Casa Colina. When I explained our situation, her positive enthusiasm made me believe that Norm could indeed learn to ski again.

In November 1997, I made December reservations for Norm and me at the Adaptive Ski School in Big Bear Lake. That gave us a month to accomplish a minor miracle. Norm had to learn about his ski gear and why he needed to wear so much clothing. Then there were his boots, their bindings, and how to balance on his skis. Deciding to start at the beginning, I piled all of Norm's ski clothing in the middle of the living room floor, then picked up one article, at a time, explaining its function, the materials it was made of, and whether it needed to be washed or dry-cleaned.

I explained that his tee shirt had a turtleneck to keep his neck warm, and that it was worn under his sweater and his coat. Norm laughed out loud when we got to the long underwear, just like a child would. I showed him their function, which he thought was very funny. When we moved on to jackets and vests, I explained the difference between a very cold day and a moderate one, and impressed upon him the need for warm gloves at all times. He studied the liners that he would need for the worst chill conditions. Then he tried on his goggles; I explained their function, and he said he liked the way they felt on his face.

Finally, we got to the sunscreen and lip ice. Various medications had left him extremely susceptible to sunburn and he'd been advised to stay out of the sun. After extensive research, I found the sunscreen that divers use, offering the maximum protection against the harmful rays. It took a very long time to get through all this — and we hadn't even gotten to the boots.

Several weeks and many repetitions later, I showed Norm the socks that went inside his boots. He was confused by the need to wear two pair, since he was incapable of imagining the cold when he was feeling warm. Once he'd sorted out the fact that the thin socks went under the thick ones, we were ready to tackle the boots, which were stiff, large, and very hard to get into. We struggled together, but got the boots buckled, and Norm stood up and tried walking around the house. "Moon walkers," he called them, as he shuffled around in the clumsy footwear, but he finally got comfortable, so we moved on to the helmet.

Before his accident, Norm never had worn head protection on the slopes, but I insisted he wear the helmet. He was willing, but had a hard time fitting it on his head, which involved stretching it out as far as it would go so it would fit his face snugly. Then there was the chin strap: Norm's coordination wasn't steady, and it took him several weeks to learn to snap the strap under his chin, something he still occasionally needs help with. Next came the goggles, which went over the helmet, the strap taped to the back. This would prevent the strap from coming off while he was moving down the mountain, something too frightening to imagine.

Last on the list was fitting Norm's boots into the bindings of his skis. I balanced him so he wouldn't fall, and my heart broke as I watched his frustration at what felt to him like a brand-new experience, even though he'd been doing it since he was four. Blazing outside our windows, the sun blinded me for a moment, which struck me funny as we stood in the living room where Norm was relearning to ski. *Only in California,* I thought, where progressive thinkers tried anything and everything. I snapped a picture of Norm, who was willing to be photographed, and, to this day, we both chuckle whenever we look at it.

Next was the toughest part: I deliberately tipped Norm over gently, time and again, showing him how to get up when he fell in his ski gear. To add to my already anxious anticipation, Norm was fifty pounds heavier now than when he'd skied in the past. He'd forgotten that food made a person gain weight, had lost all conception of fat, protein, and carbohydrates, and ate whatever he wanted, something we would remedy later. When he finally was able to dress in his gear, stand up on his skis, and balance himself, we were good to go — at least as good as we'd ever be.

Adaptive Ski School

The drive to Big Bear was a quiet one. Norm had no idea of the danger he was about to place himself in; he was simply excited and could hardly wait to get there. I, on the other hand, was drowning in dread, and almost turned back, over and over. I hated making decisions for Norm. What if this turned out badly and he ended up in even worse shape? Why couldn't he be content to stay home where it was safe and warm?

Arriving at Frank's house in Big Bear, we shared hugs and unloaded our car, and I became resigned: Norm wasn't finished with what he had to do on this earth. My job was to help him with his attitude, offer him the quality of life he deserved, and open doors to whatever he wanted to accomplish. I was his mouthpiece, his teacher, and his cheerleader, but beyond that, I needed to let go.

Bright and early in the morning, our car loaded with ski gear, we headed for the slopes. The Adaptive Ski School was in a building separate from the main lodge, and from the minute we entered the small room stacked with adaptive equipment, I knew it would be fun. The small staff of volunteers and paid instructors were smiling at everyone, busy making sure they were having a good time. I noticed a picture of a brain on the wall, separated into sections labeled "the chocolate zone," "the fun zone," and so on. Next to that was a large sign that said MOANING with a red line drawn through it. It meant NO MOANING; everyone was there to have fun, not moan or complain. I considered myself reprimanded.

While we filled out the paperwork, I learned that most of the instructors were volunteers, having completed an extensive training program before taking any disabled students on the slopes. They were a great example of people giving back, assisting the disabled in enjoying a quality of life otherwise unavailable. On the form, I paused at the line that asked for an evaluation of Norm's skiing ability. Eyes filling with tears, I breathed deeply, checked "Beginner," and turned in the paper. In a few minutes, Norm was assigned two instructors, Patty and Thomas, to stand in front of him and take up the rear.

It was the first time I'd been willing to trust others enough to place Norm in their care. But when he left the lodge with his new instructors, I was plenty nervous. *This is what they're trained for,* I told myself, watching Patty and Thomas each take one of Norm's arms. He looked radiant as the threesome approached a small hill just outside the lodge. With his instructors keeping Norm balanced, I saw them reach the top of the shallow incline, where they helped Norm get into his skis.

The tears began rolling down my face. Frank was crying, too, as we watched Norm moving back and forth on his skis, something we thought we would never witness again. I was scared, excited, and in awe, recalling the medical personnel who had suggested that my husband belonged in a convalescent home. *We showed them, didn't we?* I said silently. Norm may not have been the advanced skier he once was, but he was on his way to recovery, gaining the ability to truly enjoy his life. Wasn't that what it was all about?

Patty and Thomas herded Norm over to the ski lift. I could barely watch as they told the lift operator to stop the machinery while they got Norm situated in the chair. Slowly they rose, until they got him off the lift and stood facing the beginner's slope. The next thing I knew, they all soared down the slope together, resembling an animal with six legs, three heads, and three bodies. Amazed by Norm's courage, I watched them do it again and again while Norm got his bearings. Apparently, his lifetime of skiing was awakening in his muscle memory, and, in a few minutes, they were on their way to the intermediate mountain. My fear rose all over again. Then I recalled something I'd read when Norm was in Casa Colina: "Freedom to work, to play, to live our life without limits, to be a whole person."

Sweet Success

Norm skied all day. His attempt to get back on the slopes was a smashing success, and he was rebuilding his self-confidence, first on the bike and now on skis. He felt less isolated, and from that moment on, he and I were a dedicated team: he'd tell me what he wanted to do, and I'd find a way for him to do it.

After six more sessions at the Adaptive Ski School, we received a newsletter from Casa Colina announcing a ski outing to the same place where we had just been, the Adaptive Ski School. I read Norm the article (he still couldn't read) and he signed up for five more lessons. He continued to gain confidence as he slowly inched toward his goal — to ski Geronimo, a black-diamond run for the most advanced skiers.

On each of our ski trips, I didn't get on the slopes until Norm was safely in the hands of his instructors. Even in his compromised position, he was a much more skilled skier than I ever would be, and I didn't want to slow him down. I met some wonderful people in the lodge, particularly two gentlemen in wheelchairs. They didn't work, not because they couldn't find or hold jobs; rather, if they earned their own money, their medical benefits would be taken away. It's a crime to force people into idleness, to take away their pride and self-esteem in trade for medical benefits. Putting things right for disabled people is an uphill battle all the way, and we are still climbing.

We ended the ski season with a final trip to Lake Tahoe, to the Adaptive Ski School at Alpine Meadows. We stayed at the River Ranch Inn, next to the Truckee River. I fell soundly asleep under a cozy feather comforter. Wanting never to get up again, I awoke in the morning and gazed outside at the blanket of white covering the earth everywhere. Ending the reverie, I began helping Norm into his ski clothes. He'd become confident enough to do most things by himself at Big Bear, but now, in brand-new surroundings, he relied on me to teach him how to operate and maneuver his way around. It was like starting all over again.

We headed down to breakfast, where a long table was laden with cereal, fruit, muffins, orange juice, and coffee. I showed Norm how to handle the buffet-style meal. Looking out the windows as we sat and ate, I got seasick watching the fast-moving waters rushing over the large boulders in the river.

When we went to the car and loaded our ski equipment, the car wouldn't start. Apparently, the twenty-degree weather had affected the battery. I unloaded all the stuff from the car, wondering what we were going to do. I simply couldn't disappoint Norm; he had worked too hard to get here. I was relieved to discover that a shuttle bus from Alpine Meadows came regularly for people staying in the lodge. As it turned out, though, AAA showed up first and jump-started the car. After reloading the gear, we were on our way to Alpine Meadows.

Arriving there, I unloaded our stuff once again, but had forgotten to put our skis back in. I asked an instructor to watch Norm while I drove back, disgusted with myself. What if our skis had been stolen? But there they were, in front of the lodge where I'd left them. I loaded them onto the ski rack, drove back to the slopes, and proceeded to get Norm ready for his lesson. I was so tired by then that all I wanted to do was hand him over to his instructors and spend a few hours alone. Life had become so complicated and I was always tired, but, when we left Tahoe, we declared our trip a great success and a terrific way to start a new year.

The following season, 1998–99, Norm got stronger and more aggressive on his skis. His balance improved, and he was working on speed control, but I couldn't forget that he was constantly in danger. It was the little things, like not knowing when to get off the ski lift. On one run, his instructor got off the lift, unaware that Norm hadn't followed. He called to Norm to get off quickly, but Norm had gone too far to safely exit the lift. He needed to ride it back down and up again, but his brain hadn't told him he wasn't safe, so he jumped. The landing bruised his shoulder and his hip badly, and cut his leg right through his pants. Luckily, he didn't fall on his left side, where the defibrillator was implanted, but he was pretty beat up when we reunited in the ski lodge.

I prayed his brain had received no further damage, and told myself I couldn't continue watching Norm have accidents, but I didn't call off the trip. These were the risks Norm and I had both agreed to take to give his life meaning.

Chapter Thirteen

Behind the Wheel

Please, Not the Car!

The idea of Norm driving a car terrified me. Cycling had been frightening at first, but the worst had already happened on the bike, and I'd accepted it. Skiing had been tough to face, too; the thought of him falling and breaking a leg was unbearable, yet I'd grown accustomed to it. But the mere thought of Norm behind the wheel of a 3200-pound steel missile capable of accelerating to ninety mph made me close my eyes, shake my head, and wonder what on earth was coming next.

It was just too soon for driving. At that point Norm's lessons were all about making the necessary mistakes that would finally set him on his path to freedom. Cycling and skiing held the potential for him to get hurt and suffer additional disabilities, but he had some wiggle room to move the wrong way or to forget himself for a moment. Mistakes on a bike or skis didn't necessarily mean death or putting someone else in harm's way. Driving, however, could be lethal to Norm if he forgot which way he was going, or what a certain pedal was for, and it was equally hazardous to others. What if he hit someone, or was hit, when he lost track of right and left, a confusion that often occurred in his day-to-day life?

No, driving was something else altogether, and when he started asking about it, I clenched my teeth and took the only approach I could at the moment: ignore, ignore, ignore. I didn't want to deprive my husband of an independent life. Quite the opposite; I was fed up with driving him everywhere, performing double duty for his doctors' appointments, haircuts, schooling, and all the rest. I wanted him to have his freedom as much as I wanted my own life back, but I wasn't willing to let him kill himself getting there.

"How come I'm not driving, Dora?" he would ask. "What do I need to do to get my driver's license back?" And, of course, he never stopped asking.

"But you don't like driving," I reminded him. He really didn't, and he'd pulled some pretty creative stunts to get out of it. Before his brain injury, just as we were getting ready to leave to visit friends, grocery shop, or go to dinner, he would suddenly have a backache or a sore foot, or his arm would hurt, allegedly rendering him incapable of taking the wheel. I'd come to accept this and never minded doing the driving.

"Why the turnabout now?" I wanted to ask him, but I already knew the pattern. It was all about personal freedom, and when Norm wanted to learn something, yearning to feel freedom of motion and a sense of independence, he'd latch onto it with everything he had and wouldn't let go. It was just like when he felt driven to ski and ride his bike, and had pestered me relentlessly to help him relearn those skills.

Now, it was the car. He knew from experience that I had acquiesced to each of his desires and he had done well with them. Apparently, Norm realized that he hadn't lost his ability to get what he wanted by never letting up. But driving a car? Ever since Norm's brain injury, I'd been nurse and facilitator, extremely protective of him and always trying to keep him safe. As a result, I tried to avoid finding him risky new adventures, even if he'd done them before.

In contrast, Norm seemed to thrive on conquering the things that had once been second nature. I knew that his indomitable attitude was part of his former personality, which was all well and good when he had his wits about him, but with ABI, he no longer knew the status of his current abilities, and wasn't aware of what made him safe. I stood my ground, and the car remained off limits for a time, but I knew it was just a matter of time before Norm would tackle this dangerous thing. And no matter how I felt about it, I would be there, figuring out how to help him succeed.

Phase One

As the weeks went by, I discussed the situation with Norm's therapists. Apparently, men with brain injuries felt that driving was a part of their masculinity, while women didn't relate to it as essential to their femininity. Thus it was inevitable that Norm would want to get behind the wheel. But how would I go about making it happen? Clearly incapable of making such a serious decision myself, I needed to create a plan that allowed me to leave it to the experts. If Norm tested well, it was less dangerous than I thought; if he tested poorly, the decision would be made for him, letting me off the hook.

I stuck to my assertion that it was too soon for Norm to drive, but I had to look into it. What if he sneaked around, found the keys, and took a spin by himself? I had considerations beyond his ability to remember which pedal was which and how much speed felt safe. What if his defibrillator went off while he was driving? I'd never heard of anyone with an ICD having problems in the car. The doctors had never mentioned it. Was that because they believed it wouldn't affect him, or because he'd been in such bad shape that the thought of him driving hadn't even occurred to them? It was a frightening dilemma. I hoped Norm wouldn't pass his evaluation, but I didn't want him to be demoralized or embarrassed, so I continued searching for assistance. I needed to help him prepare for the test, but how?

Norm's primary therapist at Glendale Adventist Medical Center had a suggestion: she told me that Northridge Medical Center offered a driving program called "Driver Preparation." When I called, voice shaking, to ask for what I wanted, someone informed me that Faye, the program coordinator, would send a stack of forms to fill out. There would also be materials to read about the program, which provided a car for evaluation and driver training to individuals who've suffered injury, illness, or a condition that may have affected their ability to drive. They catered to people with all kinds of limitations — physical, cognitive, visual, or perceptual. A copy of their initial report would be sent to the DMV and the doctor. Only after Norm's physician completed a medical evaluation and suggested driving for his patient, was Norm eligible for the program. Weeks went by before Northridge Hospital received the extensive paperwork from Norm's doctor and the hospital called to make an appointment for us to meet Faye.

The initial evaluation comprised two elements: a clinical part, done by an occupational therapist specially trained in the field of comprehensive driving tests, and a "behind the wheel" evaluation of a person's actual driving skills in a variety of traffic conditions, conducted by an occupational therapist and a driving instructor. I relaxed a bit when I was told that the test car had an instructor's accelerator and brake. This meant that the instructor could take control whenever necessary, so I stopped imagining Norm getting in a terrible accident and injuring his instructors in the process.

Waiting in the outer office while Faye put Norm through a battery of tests to determine his comprehension, vision, mobility, and reaction time, I was relatively calm, certain that Norm wouldn't be given the go-ahead. I considered how different it would be in a year or two. Maybe we could revisit it then. After three hours of testing, Norm emerged from Faye's office mentally exhausted but smiling. Faye walked out after him, announcing that he'd successfully completed phase one. Wasn't I happy for him, and when did I want to bring him in for the second phase — driving on the road? I forced a smile and made an appointment for one week hence, wondering how I'd get any sleep in the meantime.

Phase Two

W hile I tried not to think about what was coming, Norm was like a kid waiting for Christmas. It was a busy week of self-talk as I worked through my anxiety. I still didn't have a handle on my feelings the following week when we arrived at Northridge Medical Center for phase two. Norm was about to get behind the wheel of a car and would be driving on the road again. I pulled up to the hospital, hit the button, and a machine spat out a parking receipt, as if in slow motion. It was early in the day when we walked to the front door of the hospital. *If only the sky would open up,* I thought, *and cause some natural disaster, that might allow Norm to avoid causing one of his own.*

The large glass doors automatically opened as we walked to the elevators. No disasters today. Norm pressed the UP button while I tried to figure out how I could take him back home again. We got off on the third floor as planned, and the receptionist asked us to be seated. Reality had sobered me beyond my ability to pretend as we waited for our names to be called.

I grabbed a magazine and tried to read, watching Norm, who wasn't at all nervous. I expected that he simply believed he could drive because he had done it before. There was no doubt in his mind that he'd pass the test. I was happy for his self-confidence, but I knew that he had absolutely no idea what he could or couldn't do. It was my job to keep him safe, and I wasn't sure I was doing it all that well. These kinds of fears and problems would remain a source of anxiety, a continual challenging search concerning what was right for Norm and what wasn't.

I studied the other people in the waiting area. Many of them were in wheelchairs or had a metal halo surrounding their heads, indicative of particular types of brain injury. As I listened to their various conversations and considered the obstacles they faced, I realized that Norm and I were lucky. The literature in the giveaway bins told me that some people would receive free authorization from the Department of Rehabilitation if this program would allow them to return to work. Norm didn't fall into that category; he was a long way from returning to work as a corporate vice president, but our health insurance would cover some of the costs.

They finally called our names and we walked into Faye's office. There we met Lawrence, a pleasant, soft-spoken middle-aged man who would be Norm's driving instructor. When Faye said it was time to start, I stood there unable to move. *Faye has been doing this for years,* I told myself. *She's successful at her job.* When Lawrence said that all of his students had eventually passed the DMV test, I had mixed emotions, wanting Norm to triumph and wishing he wouldn't. We were soon heading for the elevator, taking us to the hospital lobby and the dark green Chevy sedan that was waiting just outside.

I watched them pull away, Lawrence driving, Norm riding shotgun, and Faye in the back. I waved weakly and headed straight to a nearby Denny's; I had two hours to waste over pancakes, coffee, and orange juice. When I couldn't sit there any longer, I went back to the hospital lobby. The Chevy pulled up, Lawrence at the wheel. I ran out to meet them, and there stood Norm, relaxed and happy, chatting with his instructors about the ride.

"He did very well for his first time," Lawrence told me. "We're looking forward to the next one." I stared at Norm, who was all in one piece. Nothing terrible had happened; in fact, it looked like nothing even remotely amiss had occurred. The lessons continued over the next year, the instructors continuing to evaluate Norm's progression, but six months into Norm's training, Faye told Norm that he wasn't progressing. She suggested he stop the lessons and continue to let his brain heal. "In about six months," she said, "you can come back and try again."

"But if I don't drive now," Norm said, "how will I ever learn?"

This was the first time since the accident that I'd seen Norm stand up for himself. And he made sense, his argument so convincing that Faye agreed to let him continue until the next formal evaluation. For me, it was the same old conflict between pride that Norm had the self-esteem to argue, and fear that he would get himself hurt or killed.

We fell into a routine: three days a week, we'd travel the forty miles to Northridge and Norm would go driving with Lawrence. I was away from the house most of the day, and bills, cleaning, errands, and yard work were piling up. As much time and money as his driving efforts were costing us, Norm was adamant, and I did not get in his way — even when Lawrence and Faye agreed that he wasn't yet ready to be evaluated by the DMV. Norm wouldn't take no for an answer; he declared that he was going to try, no matter what anyone thought.

It was as if he'd put both feet into wet cement and refused to budge. His commitment was aggressive and relentless and I knew nothing would stop him. Though Norm and I didn't always agree on time frames, I'd noticed that the times when I'd let him have his way, he experienced some of his most stunning successes.

Shortly after his declaration, Norm called the DMV himself and scheduled an evaluation in El Segundo, near Los Angeles. At first he didn't pass the written test, due to his inability to read and comprehend the material. But when he got someone to read the questions to him, he missed only two, which allowed him to go forward. It seemed that his ability to read questions and answer them was irrelevant; what mattered was his understanding of the rules of the road and his ability to read and comprehend the one-word posted signs. He passed that test with flying colors, and I was delighted for him.

Later, when we scheduled his actual driving test, we were told that his defibrillator would have no impact on his driving ability. So, the day we headed for the DMV for Norm's road test, I used self-talk. *What will I do,* I asked, *if he doesn't pass the test? Drive him around for the rest of our lives?* I needed to let go and allow the DMV to make the final decision. And I needed to root for my husband, no matter how frightened I felt.

We headed into the DMV chaos, long curving lines of impatient people spilling out the door and down the front walkway. We passed everyone, since Norm would be evaluated by a specialty department, and sat for only a few minutes before a tall gray-haired gentleman asked Norm to follow him to our car. When they took off, I walked in circles around the parking lot, confused as to what I wanted to hear on their return. The upshot was that Norm had been right: he was ready to drive, and proved it by passing the test. So, in the spirit of Willie Nelson, Norm was "On the Road Again."

Today, Norm drives himself to the grocery store, the movie theater, and the golf course. His problem isn't with driving itself; it's his short-term memory, which confounds him when he tries to get back home. I came up with some creative ways for Norm to find his way around. Each time he goes to a new place, I go with him the first time, pointing out landmarks and using repetition to imprint the route in his mind. Eventually, when he's able to get there and back without coaching, I let him go alone. It works.

Why don't we just install a GPS navigating system in our car? We already have one, but Norm doesn't use it, because he can't focus on two things at once. When he drives, he needs to stay completely attentive to the road; and finding his way must take second place in importance. He's fine with that, and is content to drive locally. At last, I'm content as well.

Chapter Fourteen

The Blind
Leading the Blind

Top Dog

W e were sitting in the waiting room at Glendale Adventist before a therapy session when Norm looked at me and calmly said, "I want to go back to work."

Technically, he was on a one-year leave of absence from his job at the research and development company, but there was no way he was going back. He knew he couldn't work in the way he did before, and he wouldn't accept a permanent position below that of vice president. He'd taken a year-long consulting job with the same firm, since it would involve attending meetings at the corporate level, but he was unable to fulfill that contract, as his recovery had progressed more slowly than he'd expected.

Now, as his condition continued to improve, his thoughts turned to his new life. Norm's therapy at Glendale Adventist was coming to an end, and he didn't know what was next. He had always enjoyed working with people; they responded to him positively and he knew how to get the best out of everyone. When he told me he wanted to help others who were going through the same thing he'd endured, I wasn't surprised. But where would I find what he wanted?

As it happened, there was a volunteer department just down the hall. After Norm's session, we headed to an office where I told the receptionist that Norm wanted to volunteer. Polite and knowledgeable about the program, the young woman handed us a stack of paperwork (what else was new?), and we made an appointment for the following week to see Valerie, the director. She would be the one to determine Norm's strengths and to discuss available jobs and placement.

Norm was excited as we completed the forms together that night, but his confidence was low, and he was also afraid that he might not qualify and would embarrass himself. As we discussed the interview and all that he might encounter, I encouraged him to go forward. "Just do the best you can," I told him. I felt that if he got this job, he might gain the self-assurance he needed to keep trying new things. If he didn't get the job… well, we'd cross that bridge if we had to.

"What kind of job should I ask for?" Norm asked me as we headed down the freeway to Glendale.

"Let's just listen to Valerie," I said, "and see what she suggests."

He smiled. My heart swelled at his courage. He was ready to meet the challenge.

The elevator door opened beside a rushing water fountain in which red, yellow, and white flowers bloomed. A good omen. Once we were inside the volunteer office, Valerie, a beautiful dark-haired woman with a warm smile on her face, greeted us. "You must be Norm and Dora," she said, extending her hand as she invited us in to her tiny inner office.

We sat at a small round table, and Valerie asked Norm about his background and why he wanted to volunteer. He filled her in about his heart attack and resulting brain injury. "I want to help other people who have to go through this," he stated quite simply. She asked him about his likes and dislikes and how he felt about animals. Norm told her about all the dogs he had owned. "I never met a dog I didn't like," he said, which seemed to please Valerie.

She explained their "Top Dog" program, which involved using dogs for therapy. A woman named Cheryl, who owned two shiatzus named Charlie and Princess, had started the program years ago. She would walk from hospital room to hospital room with her dogs, allowing patients to pet them. The patients' faces would light up as they forgot their sorrows and pains for a few moments, and their frowns became big smiles.

Norm responded immediately, sensing this was something he could do, since he loved dogs so much. Valerie sent him downstairs to get his picture taken for the badge he needed to wear around his neck whenever he was working. The next step was to go to the hospital store and buy him a blue uniform jacket, which he'd wear with white pants and tennis shoes.

"You're going to look so handsome in your uniform," I teased. "You'd better watch out, you're going to attract all the ladies' attention."

He smiled happily. Our last stop was at the lab to get him a TB test, required for anyone spending time with patients. When we headed home that evening, Norm felt like he was returning to some kind of normal life.

In a few days, we met Cheryl, a middle-aged woman with auburn hair and lovely skin. I was relieved to find her so patient and kind as she helped Norm get used to his new job. Because of Norm's short-term memory problems, he would never have been able to find his way around the hospital if Cheryl hadn't agreed to help him. "It really feels good to be working again," Norm said with satisfaction at the end of his first day's orientation. That was exactly what I wanted to hear.

Our next meeting included Cheryl, an assistant named Bill, and, finally, the dogs. They were beautifully groomed with pink bows tied on their heads. When Norm leaned down and kissed them, the long hair on their tails swished excitedly from side to side at the attention. I waved, watching Cheryl, Bill, and Norm head down the hall with the two dogs in a basket on wheels. When I picked Norm up at the end of the day, he said he'd been sad to see the sick people, but he was thrilled by how well they responded to the dogs.

Things were going so well that, on the sixth day, I dropped Norm off at the front door of the hospital and told him he was on his own. He needed to find the office without me. He assured me that he'd get lost and I'd probably never see him again, but I prodded him forward, saying, "If you get lost, have anyone in the hospital call me and I'll come right back to pick you up." I left him, a mixture of anger, fear, and disbelief on his face that I would abandon him to the vast hallways and elevators. I drove away quite upset, but never received a call.

Having some free time when Norm was at his new job was a blessing. It had been so long since I'd just sat and read uninterruptedly for an hour. Each night when I picked Norm up, he was excited about seeing Cheryl and the dogs the next day, but his enthusiasm was short-lived. At the beginning of the third week, he told me he loved them all but had become bored.

I'd known this would happen, but had hoped it would last at least six months. When Norm said goodbye to Cheryl, telling her he was ready for a more challenging assignment, she was sad to see him go. She wished him good luck in his next endeavor, and I took him home, wondering what form that endeavor would take.

Brainstormers

Valerie was surprised that Norm was looking for a new job so soon. She told him he had done a good job and she would find him something else to do. I suggested that was in keeping with Norm's goal to help others in his circumstances. I'd searched high and low for a brain-injury support group for Norm and me right after the accident, but had come up empty. *Why not start one of our own?* I thought. True, neither of us had ever run a support group before, but we both knew how to run a business meeting. We could start there. It would be one foot in front of the other, the blind leading the blind, but it was the only thing that came to mind.

Thankfully, Norm thought it was a good idea that would help him reach his goal. The nearest support group for brain-injury survivors was about forty miles from our home, which was too far. We called Teresa, Norm's former therapist, to share our idea, and she agreed to help us investigate the possibilities. On August 18, 1998, we received a memo from the director of rehabilitation telling us she would be happy to lend her support in running this group through the Communicative Disorders Department of Glendale Adventist Hospital, assisting us in any way possible.

First things first, I thought, opening the dictionary to find a name for our new group, something not only descriptive but also motivating. I found twenty-one dictionary entries with "brain" as their prefix, stopping at the word "brainstorming." The definition was "to engage in or organize shared problem solving." That was perfect — it was exactly what we would be doing, solving problems as a group in an organized way.

Now that we had our name, "The Brainstormers," we needed to get the word out. Teresa contacted the hospital media department, which released an article in the *Glendale News,* announcing the group, whom it was for, and when we would meet. After deciding to hold the meetings on the second and last Wednesday of each month, we distributed fliers and gave the information to the California Head Injury Foundation for publication in their newsletter. We talked about making name badges for each prospective group member, a crucial detail, since most people suffering with ABI had little or no short-term memory and wouldn't remember each other's names from one meeting to the next. It seemed like we were well on our way.

With little idea of what to do, I moved forward, certain only that this group was the next logical step for Norm and me. During the two weeks before we started, we visited two existing brain-injury support groups to see what they were doing and what worked. The first, at Casa Colina, was facilitated by a social worker, while the second, at Northridge Hospital, had no designated facilitator. After both meetings Norm and I agreed that we didn't really like either one. The first was too structured and the second too uncertain. Just like the Three Bears, we wanted to create a group that was neither too hot nor too cold. It needed to be just right, and I didn't yet know exactly what that meant. I knew only that, while we would concentrate on the brain-injured individuals, I wanted to include their caregivers, who had no support system whatsoever. I figured the meetings would determine the agendas, but planned to invite caregivers and family members, crucial participants in a brain-injured person's support system.

My only experience with brain injury so far was with Norm, who apparently was considered a high-functioning person. I could only imagine what kinds of cases would come in the door, but kept an open mind, trusting that the right people would show up. Our goal, as stated on our fliers, was to discuss day-to-day situations that arose, exchanging information that would help improve our members' quality of life. The best part was that Norm would facilitate the group and encourage participants to raise the subjects they wanted to discuss.

The First Meeting

Norm and I showed up at the first meeting with a prepared agenda. We sat at the table and watched a few people walk in, apparently with no idea where they were going. The baffled look on their faces told me they were in the right place, and we greeted our five original members that day, congratulated them on finding us, and invited them to take a seat. We had decided to start by having each person introduce him- or herself and talk about how they had sustained their brain injury.

Someone had had a stroke, another an ear infection, and yet another had suffered a heart attack, like Norm. It was fine for the first meeting, but I soon stopped this practice when I learned that focusing on the present was far more productive than rehashing the past. It was all trial and error, but this was what we had to do, and Norm and I both knew it.

I suggested to Norm that we spend the first year focusing on ABI education, since we all needed information more than anything. When he agreed, I scheduled speakers who informed us on subjects like social security, neuropsychology, driving, and nutrition, etc. This was a big hit with everyone, as they were finally getting answers to questions they'd been asking for a long time. I created a list of names and phone numbers of all the group members, and established what I called "Group Ground Rules," basic behavior points, like no interrupting when someone was speaking, no criticizing, and constant encouragement. The day before each meeting, I printed up an agenda, so the members could think about what we'd be covering.

It was going pretty well, considering that I didn't know what I was doing, but I was having trouble getting printed material from the Brain Injury Association. When nothing materialized after a third phone call, I ordered their book, *Helping Ourselves,* a small guide for brain-injury support groups. It wasn't much, but it was the only document I could get. Basically, I was on my own, something I'd grown accustomed to, and I carried on, mostly because it meant so much to Norm.

The meetings were successful for everyone; they were leaning about their current conditions, an important step for ABI recovery, and they were making friends with others who were facing the same challenges. Pretty soon we got referrals from several hospitals, and grew from five to ten members in the first year.

I was constantly impressed with how much the members could do on their own: driving, cooking, cleaning, and self-care. I decided to add food to our agenda, even though *Helping Ourselves* advised against it. I'd always enjoyed a snack at a meeting, and I wanted to give our group something of a party atmosphere. It definitely changed things; everyone liked it, and now we all take turns providing refreshments.

Field Trips

After the first year, the members had gotten to know each other and would talk on the phone between meetings, but it was apparent that they had few outside activities. In light of their having made so much progress, the best gift I could give them was to focus the second year on socialization. Up to now, I knew only what each person with ABI wanted me to know about him or her. They were relatively self-sufficient, finding their way to the meeting room each week and getting to the rest rooms and back, but on our first outing, to the IMAX theater downtown, I was in for a rude awakening.

We met at Glendale Adventist Hospital and got on a bus to take us downtown. Everyone was excited and ready to have fun as we headed onto the freeway. The drive was unremarkable, and I felt confident when we piled out in front of the ticket booth. Each person held his or her own money, but it took only seconds for me to realize that most of them had no idea how much was in their hands. They stepped up to the booth and started counting their pennies, accepting my help. The ticket sellers were relieved when we finally got inside the theater, leaving a long line of frustrated people behind us. No one in the group seemed to care, but I came away with a few more gray hairs and a better understanding of my group members' abilities, or lack thereof.

I discovered that they had hidden their limitations from me: some of them couldn't cross the street; others had never seen a buffet lunch, or were unable to read a menu, find their way to and from the rest rooms, or figure out how to pay for their meals. We still managed to have a good time, but we had a lot of work to do.

Instead of giving up on field trips, I scheduled twelve over the next year, including the Japanese Gardens in Sherman Oaks, the Hollywood Bowl, lawn bowling, and the Getty Museum. I had each person fill out a medical form, so that if anything happened to them I could contact family members and give emergency information when needed.

The next task was to put some strategies in place to help them cope with their individual disabilities. Often, I noticed that brain-injury people had trouble dealing with the whole of something. Breaking things down into sections and categories usually worked, so I grabbed some takeout menus from a few local restaurants and brought them to the group. I divided the food choices into categories, like soups, sandwiches, and salads. If they were hungry for a sandwich, I showed them how to block out the rest of the menu and consider only the sandwich selections. Also, I had them pay me right there in the meeting room, so they could learn to handle money. It was very time consuming, but this was the only way for them to learn.

My biggest disappointment was that no caregivers showed up for our outings, but I understood. They were all overwhelmed, perhaps with jobs and children to care for, while they dealt with their brain-injured loved ones. I never stopped learning from the group; I called them "my heroes" because they all made major strides toward recovery.

The group has grown to thirty members now, and we have become a family. To this day, I'm unable to define my job description; I try to do everything, from finding lawyers, food, housing, medical help, counseling, social services, financial guidance, and transportation, to defending them when they can't defend themselves. Despite their problems and deficiencies, they're fighters, with gentle souls and tremendous courage, and are a constant source of inspiration.

Caregivers

The brain-injured folk are being somewhat taken care of, but I still despair at the plight of the caregivers. Some of them attend our meetings regularly, getting educated about ABI and learning where to get help for their loved ones, but they never get a chance to air their own sorrows. Many feel that with a loved one in such dire straits, they have neither the time nor the right to get support for themselves. They certainly can't bring it up in front of their loved ones, who wouldn't be able to understand, and they need to appear strong for the people who are relying on them.

Since I can't do it myself, I strongly urge caregivers to start support groups for themselves as soon as possible. The caregiver has his or her own trauma to deal with, and without a caregiver, a person with brain injury would be lost. During the year following Norm's heart attack, I slept one to two hours a night, gained fifty pounds, and felt like my only reason to live was to nurse Norm. I didn't get my hair cut or my nails done, and when I had any time that wasn't filled with Norm's needs, I slept.

One day, I looked in the mirror — a practice I had deliberately stopped — and saw a haggard old woman staring back at me. She had aged twenty years, her thinning hair was straight and oily, her pants didn't fit her waist anymore, and her nails were short and broken. A visit to the hairdresser and manicurist did a world of good, as did getting on a sensible eating plan. I watched the weight drop off (never enough, of course), and was determined not to let such decline recur.

Caregivers, please remember that your health is as important to your loved one as it is to you. Eventually, I joined a group for caregivers who had loved ones dying from a variety of diseases. It wasn't exactly what I needed; no one there knew anything about brain injury, and my loved one wasn't dying, but trying to figure out how to go on living. Still, it was better than nothing. I remained in the group for only a year, but it felt good to vent my feelings.

If you can't find an actual brain injury caregivers' support group, any group that deals with the multifaceted adventure called care-giving will have something to offer you. I have no referrals for ABI caregivers as yet, but it's only a matter of time. The need grows in direct proportion to the growth of the disability, making it important for all of us to learn how to survive not only ABI itself, but also the ordeal of caring for the brain injured.

Chapter Fifteen

Brainstorming

Breaking the Silence

During the early years of our support group, I learned much more from the Brainstormers than I could have imagined. I tried to put myself in their shoes, impossible though it was, and see the world from their point of view. It was a continual amazement.

For example, one Wednesday afternoon about a half-hour before the meeting was set to begin, a middle-aged woman haltingly stepped into the room. Her eyes darted nervously, and, in an almost imperceptible voice, she asked, Is this the brain injury meeting?"

I told her it was and introduced myself. She said her name was Irene.

"I need you to know," Irene said shyly, "that ever since my brain injury, I can't tolerate noise — regular noise, like ringing phones or a watch alarm." She couldn't be in spaces that had piped-in background music, and television was out of the question, because her brain had lost its ability to filter sound. Imagine every instrument in a symphony orchestra all playing at the same time as loudly as possible. That was how the world sounded to Irene every day; any sound her brain picked up bombarded her at a painfully high decibel level, rendering her unable to distinguish one sound from another. I asked how I could help, not entirely surprised at her condition, because someone else in our group, Madeline, reported a similar problem.

Irene showed me how to set up the room, making a space for her in the corner most shielded from sound. When Madeline arrived, I introduced them. Madeline told Irene that an audiologist had prescribed an earpiece that filters sounds for her. She wears it all the time, and she can watch TV, go to the movies, and tolerate large groups of people who are talking simultaneously. Irene was grateful to learn something her doctor hadn't told her, and I was thrilled to see the Brainstormers helping each other. It was a beautiful example of how much meaning our support group holds for each of us.

In the group, we learned how each member had sustained his or her injuries, and I worked to understand the unique challenges each person faced. Florence, a victim of domestic violence, had been struck on the head by her husband. The police took her to the emergency room, but, after several tests, she was sent home with a clean bill of health.

Florence was relieved, but, as time passed, she realized that her brain would shut down for minutes at a time while someone was speaking to her. When the gap ended and she was again able to hear the person talking, she had missed the information, which limited her comprehension. She went into hiding, afraid it would happen again, but this was impractical because she had a small child to raise. She continues to see doctors who she hopes will give her a diagnosis, but she's still waiting. At least Florence has the group, where she can vent her frustrations and get practical advice about how to cope with her episodes.

Gail began attending Brainstormers shortly after sustaining her brain injury from an aneurysm — a ruptured blood vessel. Her speech was so badly affected that each time she tried to speak, she'd stutter until a single word painfully fought its way out of her mouth. Although she continued coming to meetings, she kept quiet — until one afternoon.

As usual, we went around the room, everyone taking a turn to discuss what had arisen for them since our last meeting. When it was Gail's turn, she opened her mouth and spoke with ease and clarity, no hesitation, no stuttering. My mouth fell open, as did everyone else's around the table.

"What happened to you?" I asked. "What do you think has caused so much improvement?"

"I had a seizure last week," she said without pause or stutter, "and the doctor changed my medications. I started taking something called vitamin O, and I'm feeling great." Gail had been struggling for so long, but now, with a newfound ability to express herself, her entire life was about to change, as a variety of new opportunities became available to her.

The next week, Gail brought in written literature about vitamin O, and we all learned that this mysterious vitamin was a rich source of stabilized oxygen molecules. As yet, the FDA hasn't evaluated or rated this oxygen source, so I'm neither touting it, nor trying to diagnose, treat, cure, or prevent any kind of disease. I'm simply pointing out the value of sharing information among our group members.

The challenges of brain-injured people's lives don't prevent them from having complaints and opinions, just like everyone else. When circumstances caused me to miss a meeting, I received a call from one of the facilitators. "You have to do something about Ally," he said. "Her cussing upsets some of the members so much, they're threatening to stop attending the meetings."

While Ally was working on a film crew, someone trimmed a tree on the set, and a heavy branch fell on Ally's head, causing brain injury. I contacted Gwen, the speech and language pathologist at Glendale Adventist, and told her about Ally. Gwen had encountered this situation before, in which the person doing the swearing had no control over what he or she was saying. In Ally's case, the words just popped out of her mouth before she had a chance to rethink them. Gwen agreed to attend the next meeting and explain this to the other group members, but they weren't impressed. They understood a little better why Ally was doing it, but the consensus was that she should try to clean up her language. She said she'd try her best. It struck me as ironic that brain-injured people had trouble understanding each other's limitations. How would a healthy person ever be able to embrace the implications of this humiliating incapacity?

Mary Anne, the most recent addition to our group, sustained ABI during an operation to remove a brain tumor. It was wrapped around her optical nerve, and, when they removed it, she lost her eyesight. Now she is brain injured and blind. When people in our group start feeling sorry for themselves, Mary Anne's smile is a beacon of light and a reminder that, bad as things are, they could be a lot worse.

Kurt, a twenty-five-year-old Brainstormer, suffered his injury nearly two years earlier. In 2001 he had graduated from UC Irvine with a degree in biology, and, after working in sales for a while, moved to his parents' home to save some money while he studied to take the Dental Admission Test. Returning home one night after studying in the library, Kurt collapsed. His mother found him on the floor, passed out and struggling for breath. Stricken with encephalitis (an inflammation of the brain tissue), he lay in a coma in the hospital for several days. When he awoke, he had suffered ABI. Beyond that, there's no information about what happened, but the end result was an injured brain, and Kurt has to learn to live with it.

We discovered that his memory and topographical orientation were severely impaired, and he has come up with some ingenious strategies to accommodate himself to life. He purchased a digital camera, the Casio Exilim EX-Z, which he uses as a secondary memory — a fail-safe when there's something critical to remember. He photographs a building or the location or appearance of something, so he can constantly refresh his memory and recall the needed information. Otherwise, he could walk aimlessly around parking structures, malls, and shopping centers for hours before remembering and finding what he was looking for. The camera is small, fits in his pocket, and has a strong zoom and a large LCD screen for better viewing. He also uses a Pocket PC, the Toshiba E750, with a calendar, to make notes about his daily activities and schedule appointments. A GPS receiver that he got from the Department of Rehabilitation, and mapping software that works with his PC also make his life simpler. Of course, each person with ABI has his or her individual experience. Norm uses a paper calendar because he finds it easier, but the point is that each individual needs to find the things that will keep him- or herself organized and arriving at places on time.

Kurt uses a device from Sharper Image that contains key rings that beep when you push a button on a larger remote. You place the locator on whatever device you might need to retrieve, such as a pair of eyeglasses or a book. Then, if you can't find it, you push a button on the remote and the missing article buzzes. There are so many ways to help your loved one live an easier life, and with a little investigation, they can make your life easier, too. The bottom line is always the same: You can deal with almost any problem once you learn to think creatively.

Knowing What You Know

The most important lesson I've learned from the group is this:
When You Have a Brain Injury, You Don't Know What You Don't Know.
In a way, the inability to assess one's own safety and appropriateness in any situation is the most difficult part of dealing with brain injury. As I continued to watch and listen to the heroic people with whom I sat around a

table each week, I couldn't help wondering why these people had been singled out, along with my husband, to be victims of chance. Now, they were destined to fight their way back into a world they could no longer understand. I wanted to pity them but I knew better; they had become my teachers, and I was there to serve them and to learn. Pity was the last thing my group members needed; a good dose of self-esteem and a renewed sense of humor was the best gift they could ever receive.

Self-esteem is precisely what they needed when some of the people had to appear before an evaluation board to receive state compensation for their injuries. The worst challenge for brain-injured people is being required to prove that they have a brain injury so they can be reimbursed or compensated through their insurance. In most cases of people with ABI, there is no visible physical damage to substantiate the injury, because it's hidden inside their skulls. Often, an MRI or CT scan doesn't reveal the problem either, so they have to be questioned. This is tricky, because most people with ABI figure out how to pass as healthy just to manage their lives, and how to answer the questions the board might put to them. But, as capable as they might appear, deeper probing will reveal the lack of substance in their answers to certain questions.

For example, one of our members was asked if he could cook for himself. "Yes," he replied with a heartrending degree of self-pride. Further questioning, had there been any, would have revealed the fact that his home-cooked meals consisted of cold cereal, candy bars, crackers, and cheese. Any food preparation requiring a recipe, a stove, or reading directions was impossible. He was just so ashamed of his deficiency that he couldn't bear to tell the truth, and I couldn't bear to force him to tell the truth, even if it meant being compensated for his diminished abilities.

Laundry is another task that 90 percent of our group can't do. If you asked, they might say they can do laundry, and they can in fact throw clothes into the washing machine and push buttons; sorting colors and whites, however, is completely beyond most people with ABI.

Then there are the finances. The bills arrive, brain injury or no. If you can't read, you don't know you owe money, and if the utilities get shut off, as has often happened, the debt goes to collection, the car gets repossessed, and so on. It's all but impossible for any of us to understand what brain-injured people face daily.

So, the task of proving brain injury to a room full of uninformed people must be accomplished successfully before a person with ABI can get the financial or medical help that is rightfully his or hers. How can laymen ever understand that you don't really get their questions, and that, no matter what the MRI says, you're barely making it from one day to the next? No matter if the petitioner fights, screams and kicks — the board won't believe there's a brain injury unless they're shown documentation for every bit of it.

I recently attended an arbitration meeting for one Brainstormer who, before her evaluation, dug through her files with all her family members for weeks. She arrived with photos, letters, certificates, project examples, school grades, and notes from the school. She sat there, terrified, while a cold-hearted panel started poring over her past. This was more important than anything she had done since her injury; after all, their decision would impact whether she lived the rest of her life in a negative or positive way. The final decision hasn't yet been made, but I think she has a good chance.

So, the question hangs, unanswered. Exactly what does a person who has a brain injury look like? A good example of how deceptive this is occurred when Norm and I went skiing at the adaptive ski school one winter. As his assistant I was allowed free entrance. When we stepped up to the window where I would receive a free pass, they looked from Norm to me and asked suspiciously, "Who is disabled here?" Since Norm and I looked equally healthy, they thought we were trying to cheat them out of a free ticket.

Thank God Norm hasn't lost his sense of humor. He started walking oddly and pretended to be having a seizure. "Now do I look like someone with a disability?" he asked. "Believe me, I have a brain injury, but how do you think I should look?"

They handed me my pass and were relieved when we moved away from the window. We were relieved, too! As we headed for the lift, I vowed that the next time we arrived at the mountain, I'd be holding a document from Norm's doctor saying he has a brain injury, so he wouldn't have to endure that kind of humiliation again. I watched Norm jump off the lift and prepare to take a run down the mountain, exhilaration on his face. In the end, when we were out on the slopes with the wind chasing our backs and a fresh blanket of white powder cradling our skis, humiliation notwithstanding, it had all been worth it.

Chapter Sixteen

It's All In the Eyes

From Ph.D. to Freshman

Ever since Norm had been discharged from Casa Colina, our lives were all about school. I'd turned our dining room into a classroom after visiting a local supply store where teachers got materials for classes. The helpful storekeeper set me up with flash cards and some beginning books on letters and numbers. Also, to help Norm practice his alphabet, I bought the same kind of lined writing pads I'd used so long ago in grammar school.

Since he was making strides on the ski slopes and exercising other motor-function activities, my primary concern was to find Norm the right English tutor. In the past, I'd gotten some good responses when I placed ads at the local colleges. This time, though, none of the few people who answered my ad was quite right for our purposes.

Unsure what we would do to keep Norm's brain active, I got a call from a female tutor who sounded promising. Instead of coming to our house for an interview, however, she asked if we could meet her at the Leaning Center at Glendale College. I agreed, but as I circled the busy parking lot over and over, trying to find a parking spot, I wondered if I'd made the right choice. Norm could drive by then, but he could never have done this day after day, and I didn't want the job of getting him to school and back every day. The minute we met Kim inside the Learning Center, it was obvious to both Norm and me that we had the right match. Now I had to make it work in a practical way.

For personal safety reasons, Kim simply did not come to private homes. I understood, but how would Norm ever be able to get to the Leaning Center on his own without getting lost, and how would he ever find a place to park? I left Norm with Kim and went to the Disabled Office. There, I explained to the receptionist that Norm was unable to fight for a parking spot, find his car later, or even find the Learning Center Building. Something had to be done, because Norm couldn't attend college without their support.

When the receptionist said she couldn't help me, I just stood there, and she realized I wasn't about to leave until I found a solution to my problem. She sent me up the chain of command until a supervisor gave Norm a pass card that would allow him to use the faculty parking lot next door to the Learning Center

Mission accomplished. We scheduled our hours with Kim, and, by the time we left for home, Norm, oceanographer and Ph.D., was officially a college freshman, starting with a class called "English as a Second Language."

On Norm's first day, Kim walked into the classroom and told the students that he was new and would need help getting to the bookstore and cafeteria, etc. He would appreciate any help they could give him. At first, it was hard for him to keep up with the class, but the young student sitting next to Norm adopted him and, without being asked, helped Norm in every class.

One day, one of our Brainstormers facilitators, whom I call Norm S. to distinguish him from my Norm, told me about a friend, Rosemary, a speech pathologist at Pasadena City College (PCC). She worked at the Disabled Student Office in their Disabled Student Program and Services (DSP&S). This program takes each individual's needs into consideration, providing access to classrooms and to whatever materials or special tutoring a student requires. Each program is designed to help the student complete his or her education and set and achieve occupational goals. To qualify, a student must have a verifiable disability, a category that includes acquired brain impairments, communication disabilities, and learning and visual impairments, to name a few. Depending on need, students may be eligible for such services as testing accommodations, note takers, print enlargement, diagnostic assessment, tape-recorded texts, and tutoring. The program also provides special equipment such as adaptive computer devices.

Norm S. persuaded Norm and me to take a tour of the PCC Disabled Office, and am I glad we took the time! Norm switched over there the following semester, and, with the help of the DSP&S Program, still continues attending the ABI Support Group, the High Tech Center, and classes in tennis, history, math and many more. It turned out to be the answer to my prayers for finding the best place for Norm to relearn the skills he had lost.

He went every day, diligently sat in class, and did his best, but, as time passed, Norm was having more trouble than I'd anticipated. Sitting down to do homework, he'd read a few lines, and then his attention would wander. If I reminded him that he'd lost focus, he'd return to the book, but, within a few minutes, he was gazing elsewhere. One afternoon, when I was trying to figure out why Norm wouldn't study longer than ten minutes at a time, he complained of a headache. Were his eyes giving him trouble? I decided to have them checked again, as soon as I could find a doctor who knew something about brain injury and how it affected eyesight. Once again, the angels were with us: a friend referred us to Doctor Shannon Caruthers, a behavioral optometrist, founder of the Star Vision Center.

Vision Therapy

Doctor Caruthers had undetected vision problems while in college. She had to study longer than her colleagues, though she knew she was just as smart as they were, so what was the problem? When, years later, she was diagnosed with a vision problem and received treatment, the difference was so dramatic that she decided to pursue optometry. It was natural for her, having had firsthand experience with the frustration caused by vision problems.

Our first visit with this remarkable woman validated my sense that we were in the right place. Immediately, I learned that a "behavioral optometrist" is a doctor who is adept in visual rehabilitation after brain injury. Doctor Caruthers had spent many postgraduate years mastering the complex visual programs prescribed to prevent or eliminate visual problems and enhance visual performance. Also, I learned that, as I had surmised, the visual system is adversely affected when the brain is injured by trauma. Our former doctor hadn't known this, and had covered up his ignorance by telling us that nothing was wrong with Norm's ability to see.

Doctor Caruthers explained to us that the possible visual impairments after ABI could include loss of peripheral vision, double vision, difficulty reading (due to loss of eye movement control), or inability to fully move the eyes. Since two-thirds of all information we receive is visual, efficient visual skills are a critical part of learning. I regretted not having known about Doctor Caruthers earlier, but rejoiced that we'd found her now.

After a battery of tests such as moving both eyes, aligning, fixating, and focusing, Doctor Caruthers got some tangible results. Norm was having trouble with tracking (following a moving object smoothly and accurately with both eyes), fixation (moving from word to word), and peripheral vision (seeing what's outside the central area of focus while performing a visual task). No wonder Norm couldn't read: the information wasn't reaching his brain, and he was getting severe headaches as a result. Doctor Caruthers prescribed vision therapy three times a week for a year, to stimulate the brain and help the synapses (connections between neurons) begin to function more efficiently. The mental exercises would help Norm's brain become more efficient, engaging healthy neurons that were previously unused. Norm was resistant, however; despite our attempts to convince him of its importance to his recovery, he insisting that he wasn't yet ready to start any more therapy. Finally, a year after we'd met with this wonderful doctor, four and a half years after his brain injury, Norm announced that he was prepared to begin vision therapy.

Arriving early for his appointment, we met Pauline, a former schoolteacher, who smiled and lovingly held Norm's hand. The kind of woman who took charge, and was clearly not interested in wasting anybody's time, Pauline would be handling Norm's therapy. We followed her to a room that resembled a children's classroom. Pauline's desk was in the right-hand corner, her personal computer in the center of it. In the left-hand corner was the students' desk, on which sat a computer loaded with vision-therapy software. On the walls hung several board devices for checking peripheral vision and color problems. In all, it seemed a happy room, and Pauline made us feel comfortable.

When I asked to watch Norm's therapy session, Pauline said no, unsure how my presence might impact his progress. I wasn't used to being shut out, and we settled on my being in the room for the first ten minutes of every session. We would discuss how the homework had gone or any other concerns I had, and then I would leave. Norm began affectionately calling Pauline "the sergeant"; eventually, she softened, and let me sit in on some of his sessions.

To improve Norm's peripheral vision, he would stand in front of a board on which red dots were scattered. When Pauline started up the program, one of the dots would light up for a few seconds, then blink out, and another would come on. Norm's assignment was to keep his hand behind his ear until he saw a dot light up, then touch the lighted dot with his finger, and then put the hand back behind his ear. The results would be determined by how many dots he touched and how quickly he completed the exercise.

He also worked with special computer programs that helped his depth perception, focus, and visualization. Each session ended with his homework assignment. Once, he received a piece of paper with ten "E's" written across and ten written down the page, all facing different directions. We were to tape the paper on the wall, and Norm had to tell me which way each "E" was facing.

Another homework exercise to strengthen and stimulate left-brain activity was a chart with a list of words written in different colors. Norm's task was to look at the word and say the color of the letters, not the word that they spelled. The idea was that the right half of the brain tried to say the color, while the left half insisted on reading the word; the exercise coordinated the two.

For another method to relearn math, English, and reading skills, I bought Norm some study programs for his computer. Though he was doing much better by the time he had completed fifteen months of vision therapy, along with his computer-study program, he continued to have trouble reading and comprehending. He still adds letters to certain words he sees, or he reads the wrong word altogether, which stalls his comprehension, but I developed a reading method that allowed him to get all the way through a book with little frustration.

Camp's Reading Refresher Program

I started by choosing a book that Norm enjoyed. Then I'd buy a video of the movie made from that book, and have him watch it until he could repeat the story back to me, which proved that he could comprehend it. Then he would read the book — preferably in large print, so he wouldn't have to struggle to see the words. Also, I would buy an unabridged version of the book on audiotape, so the words he heard matched the written words exactly. Now we had the book, video, and audiotape. When I had trouble finding all three versions, I checked with Blockbuster or Borders for availability; Borders almost always came through.

Next, I looked for a tape player that was easy to operate and had a button for slowing down the voice on the audiotapes. After some research, I bought a Sony TCM-59V, which featured a tape counter, auto reverse, earphone jack, good speakers, and a function that slowed the audio voice. I taught Norm to operate it, and to use the tape counter to mark his book when he paused or stopped reading, so he didn't have to start over if he lost his place. Whenever I detected that he didn't understand what he'd just read, I asked him to stay on that page before going on to the next.

For Norm, reading short pieces, like *Chicken Soup for the Soul,* worked best. He would read aloud, and I could make sure he was reading all the words and not skipping around. During and after the story, we'd discuss it to check his comprehension. Today, we have an extensive collection of books, audiotapes, and videos, so Norm can choose what he feels like reading that day.

Although my system probably won't work for everyone, I invite you to give it a try. If you encounter a problem that's new and different, take a breath, think creatively, and don't be surprised if you come up with an original idea for your loved one. Whatever technique you choose, and however long it takes, almost anyone can learn to read, and it will make all the difference in the world to the brain-injured person's life. When Norm was finally able to read again, he was so excited that he spent hours reading, just as he had before his heart attack, and it worked wonders for his self-esteem.

I later learned about a program called Recording For the Blind and Dyslexic (RFB&D) This is a nonprofit organization that lends audio textbooks to people who, due to blindness or a reading disorder, can't effectively read standard print. They provide material on many different subjects at all educational levels. Norm couldn't have attended his history class if not for the textbooks on tape.

I was in awe as I watched Norm reading again, whetting his appetite for more and more information. As another result of his improved vision, his golf score has dropped from above 100 to the high eighties, while his self-confidence has risen accordingly.

Norm still has trouble reading and comprehending. When he started on the road to recovery he could barely speak. If you met him now, you'd have to listen very closely to detect any hesitation in his speech. He has learned to adapt by describing what he's trying to say instead of using the word. Sometimes he adds letters to words or he reads the wrong word, which causes problems with his comprehension, but he continues to make great strides, both with Doctor Caruthers's vision therapy and Camp's Reading Refresher Program. The Ph.D. turned freshman continues to grow and learn new skills, all the while getting a huge boost in self-esteem, giving his life meaning, and sparking his curiosity to learn more. Norm is the perfect model of will and determination for others who face the same degree of challenge that he does daily.

Epilogue

I'm sitting on a colorful swing chair out on the deck of our home in Big Bear Lake, sipping a glass of Merlot. It's the day after New Year's and a light snow is drifting down. Everything looks picture perfect — the tree limbs are laden with fresh snow, and a gray squirrel scampers up a towering pine, carrying a snack in his mouth.

Beyond the trees, I can see the ski runs at Bear Mountain Ski Resort in the distance, while people, small as ants, float down the feathery-looking mountains. I haven't been skiing this season, and I don't intend to for a while. I feel peaceful right now and skiing is the last thing I want to think about, but I have no choice.

★ ★ ★

Two weeks ago, while Norm was on the slopes in the early morning, I was peeling shrimp and baking my favorite apple pie for a dinner I was planning for Frank, Norm, and a few guests. I answered the phone, flour all over my hands, and heard Frank, who sounded upset. He had just received a call from the nearby hospital. Norm had been in a skiing accident and was in the emergency room. We had to get there as quickly as possible.

This is not happening again, I promised myself as I threw on some fresh clothes. But it was. Frank picked me up and we sped to the hospital, seven years to the day since Norm had suffered his near-fatal accident. I suddenly remembered that I'd left the stove on and phoned a friend to turn it off. When I put my cell phone back in my purse, my hands were trembling. How badly was Norm hurt? Had he sustained additional brain injury? Would all our hard work have been for nothing?

Frank pulled into a parking space and I rushed out of his truck. I was out of breath when I reached the emergency window, looking past the receptionist to a hallway. There was Norm, lying on a gurney, his face hidden. I pointed to him, muttering something about my husband and why I was here. She said I could go to him, but Frank would have to wait, since they allowed only one visitor at a time.

I walked toward the gurney where Norm lay. An intravenous line dripped into a vein in his left arm, and the left side of his face was badly scraped, as if from a skid burn. His entire face was swollen as was his neck, and the part of his neck area beneath his left cheek was bruised black, probably from being hit by his ski pole. It must have been a whopper of a fall to cause all those scrapes right through his helmet. His left eye, which was covered with gauze, scared me. What if he went blind in one eye, on top of everything else. Why did we ever buy this house in Big Bear?

★ ★ ★

Looking down from the deck this afternoon, the world is covered with snow. Up on the mountains, the beautiful white blanket seems to neutralize everything. The houses are sheeted with new-fallen snow, parts of their walls peeking through the whiteness. As much as Norm's second accident has upset me, I can't help but imagine being back on the mountain, the feel of the ski lift against the back of my legs as I shoot into the chair. I can feel the cold wind hit my face as the lift ushers me into the quiet zone of heavy hanging tree branches and dark clouds. I shake my head and return to reality, taking in the scene that could easily be a wintry postcard.

What is it about snow that makes me feel peaceful? I get the same feeling when I look into the ocean and see the vastness of existence. Dark clouds hover over the mountaintops, which could mean more snow. Everything changes so rapidly up here, you need to be prepared for bad weather at any time — and skiing accidents.

★ ★ ★

The paramedics had cut Norm's blue ski sweater and tee shirt from his wrist to above the elbow, exposing his arm to administer life-saving treatment. The expression on his face was one of deep confusion. He had no idea what had happened to him, and couldn't understand why I was crying.

He kept asking me, and I kept trying to stop crying, with little success. I kept repeating under my breath, "Dear God, why do we have to go through this again? Just when things were going so well."

Norm's clothing was wet all the way through. The nurse and I cut off his clothes, since he was headed for surgery to stitch up his eye. When we finally had him in a clean gown and under a heated blanket, he lay quietly, exhibiting no signs of pain. Thank God! I ran out and told Frank to go in and see his father. When he got to Norm's gurney, Frank threw a barrage of questions at him, asking him his name, where he was, and how old he was, trying to reassure himself that Norm's mind was still there. This seemed to be upsetting Norm, so a nurse advised Frank to stop talking, and he came out and let me go back in.

They had completed a CT scan before we got there, and the ER doctor said that, aside from Norm's pre-existing brain injury, everything looked about the same. This doctor, who would be doing Norm's eye surgery, was accustomed to treating broken arms and legs. What would happen if Norm's defibrillator went off during surgery? Would the doctor know what to do?

It was a tough decision to allow Norm into surgery. My first choice would have been to have him flown to Los Angeles, where our regular cardiologist and a plastic surgeon would be waiting to stitch up his eye. But the weather had changed, the medevac helicopters were grounded, and it wasn't safe to drive down the foggy mountain road. I had no choice but to let him go into surgery and pray that nothing bad would happen.

Frank and I walked on either side of Norm's gurney as they wheeled him into the surgical suite. We were both so nervous that we couldn't read magazines or eat while they were working on him. We just paced the waiting room, retracing our steps over and over.

At 4:30 P.M., an hour after Norm went in, a nurse told us that everything had gone fine. In his room, we learned that they'd put fifteen stitches under his eye, and they were pretty sure his sight wasn't affected. They'd placed a white knit cap on his head for warmth, and he kept feeling his face and head with his hands, trying to figure out what was going on. I sat beside him and spoke gently to him, seeing that he wasn't processing information as quickly as usual. I feared additional brain injury and, unfortunately, I was right.

I spent the night at the hospital with Norm. I couldn't leave him there alone, because he couldn't understand why he was there and why he had to stay in a prone position. It was too reminiscent of seven years ago, when he awoke every five minutes and tried to get out of bed to walk the halls. I kept him lying flat as much as I could; I got no sleep at all that night. The next day, after Norm had his bandages changed, we drove back home. I nearly fell asleep on the freeway, but we made it. Somehow, we always do.

★ ★ ★

I've begun shivering from the cold, so I leave the deck, walk back into the living room, and wrap myself in a furry blanket. I turn up the pellet stove and settle into my overstuffed burgundy-and-green-striped chair. It's been two weeks since Norm's fall, and though his physical injuries have healed well, he continues to have trouble processing information. When we first got back to La Crescenta, all he did for about a week was sleep, getting up only to eat, but, gradually, he's resumed taking short walks, working out, and going to the movies.

As I look up at the A-frame beams overhead, I wonder how many trees were cut down to build this beautiful ceiling. A bird is trying to get into the house through the plate glass windows, pecking at the frame, flying to the top of the windowpane, and then landing back down on the sill.

As much as I resent the fact that Norm was hurt on the nearby slope, I don't know what I'd have done without this house to lull me back to sanity. I still don't know how much Norm's brain suffered from the recent fall, but it appears that we'll have to repeat some of our hard work. I fear I don't have the stamina, but this is what living with brain injury is like — unpredictable, tragic, and finally, extraordinary progress.

All of the Brainstormers go through things like this, and we'll continue to face challenges. That's the nature of brain injury. I never know how I'll handle what arises, but I know that things could be a lot worse — the Brainstormers remind me when I see how many problems they solve each day and how far our group has come. More than 300 people have shuffled in and out of the group since its inception, and many of them have graduated from simply watching TV to attending college, driving, going to the theater, skiing, traveling, and contributing to the community.

We constantly help each other in every way that we can. I encourage them to take turns facilitating meetings, so they can feel independent and capable.

The goal is for me to back off eventually and hand the reins over to them entirely. They respond to my faith in them with great determination, and I know they'll succeed at living better, more independent lives.

As I said earlier, people with brain injury don't know what they don't know. This is certainly the case with Norm and his skiing. We have conflicting opinions on whether he'll be hitting the slopes next winter. I feel that he's given it all he has, but it's time to quit, because he lacks the visual skills necessary to stay safe. He disagrees, and continues to tell people that he *will* be on the mountain next year. I don't know how this will end, but our family can't bear up under any more brain injury. I encourage him to play golf and tennis, which are far less dangerous. It remains an open topic; we'll see what the coming year brings.

Norm continues at Pasadena City College, honing his tennis skills, working in the high-tech center, and attending their brain-injury support group. He and another member just signed up to volunteer for the local sheriff, setting out speed-awareness signs and later bringing them back to the station. Norm and I still lecture at the University of Judaism in Los Angeles, Cal State LA, Good Samaritan Hospital, and Glendale Adventist, as well as church and social groups.

After sorely neglecting myself during the past seven years, doing constant care-giving and problem solving for Norm, this book is my first real attempt at doing something for me. The writing process has been a great help in accepting my new life.

Whether a brain injury is sustained through heart attack, auto accident, ear infection, or any of a host of other causes, the challenges are the same. I hope my story serves to educate and to illustrate new and rewarding ways to think about ABI. It is my sincere hope, too, that this book, together with your instincts and open heart, will help you find solutions for living with brain injury, so you can see your loved one restore his or her independence as both of you create a brand-new life worth living.

A Caregiver's Bill of Rights

I have the right to take care of myself. This is an obligation, not an act of selfishness. It will make me capable of taking better care of my loved one.

I have the right to seek help from others even if my loved one objects. I recognize the limits of my own endurance and strength.

I have the right to maintain parts of my life that do not include the person I care for, just as I would if he or she were healthy. I know that I do everything I can for my loved one, and I have an obligation to do some things just for myself.

I have the right to get angry and depressed and to express difficult feelings when I need to.

I have the right to reject any attempt by my loved one, either conscious or unconscious, to manipulate me through guilt, anger, or depression.

I have the right to consideration, affection, forgiveness, and acceptance from my loved one in return for what I do, as long as I offer these qualities in return.

I have the right to take pride in what I'm accomplishing and to applaud the courage it sometimes takes to meet the needs of my loved one.

I have the right to protect my individuality and to make a life for myself that will sustain me in the time when my loved one no longer needs my help.

I have the right to expect and demand that, as new strides are made in finding resources to aid the physically and mentally impaired, similar strides will be made toward aiding and supporting caregivers.

I have the right to _____ .

Resources

Casa Colina Hospital for Rehabilitative Medicine
Transitional Living Services (TLC)
255 East Bonita Ave.
Pomona, CA 91769-6001
Barbara Urabe
909-596-7733 Ext. 4100
www.casacolina.org

Casa Colina Centers For Rehabilitation - Outdoor Adventures
Ann Johnson, Director
255 East Bonita Ave.
PO Box 6001
Pomona, CA 91769-6001
909-596-7733 Ext. 2200
www.casacolina.org

Centre For Neuro Skills (CNS)
16542 Ventura Blvd., Suite 500
Encino, CA 91436
818-783-3800 / 800-922-4994
www.neuroskills.com

Rehabilitation Associates Medical Group
Physical Medicine and Rehabilitation
H. Richard Adams, M.D.
2840 Long Beach Blvd., Suite 130
Long Beach, CA 90806
562-424-8111

Los Angeles Cardiology Associates - A Medical Group
David S. Cannom, M.D., Inc.
Cardiology & Clinical Electrophysiology
ICD Support Group / Bev Firth 213-977-4176
1245 Wilshire Blvd., Suite 703
Los Angeles, CA 90017
213-977-0419
dcannom@lacard.com

Medic Alert
Personal medical facts available 24 hours
2323 Colorado Ave.
Turlock, CA 95382
800-432-5378
www.medicalert.org

Bike Rentals-Santa Monica and Venice Beaches
Perry's Beach Café
8 locations on the bike path & the beach
Corporate Office 310-452-2399
www.perryscafe.com

Los Angeles Caregiver Resource Center
USC Andrus Gerontology Center
715 McClintock Ave.
Los Angeles, CA 90089-0191
213-740-8711 / 800-540-4442

Brain Injury Association
PO Box 16786
Sacramento, CA 95816-7305
916-442-1710

Glendale Adventist Medical Center
Rehabilitation: 818-409-8023
Volunteering: 818-409-8057

Brainstormers BI Support Group: 818-409-8023
1509 Wilson Terrace
Glendale, CA 91206-4007
www.GlendaleAdventist.com

Dial-A-Ride
633 East Broadway, Room 300
Glendale, CA 91206-4384
818-548-3960
www.ci.glendale.ca.us

Access Services
PO Box 71684
Transit Evaluations
Los Angeles, CA 90071-0684
323-780-9777

Young Scholar Store for Parent and Teacher
233 N. Central Ave.(near Galleria)
Glendale, CA 91206
818-246-7063

Radio Shack
Memory Voice
2027 Verdugo Blvd.
Montrose, CA 91020
818-248-3233
www.radioshack.com

Sharper Image
Key Holder/Timer with Alarm Clock, Light & Recorder
SR271
800-344-4444
www.sharperimage.com

www.beepingwallet.com

Pasadena City College
Disabled Student Programs & Services
Rosemary Scott, MA CCC, SLP
1570 E. Colorado Blvd.
Pasadena, CA 91106-2003
626-585-7127
www.paccd.cc.ca.us

CompUSA
Computer Programs
761 N. San Fernando Blvd.
Burbank, CA 91206
818-848-8588

Borders
Audio Books - Unabridged, Books, Movies
100 S. Brand Blvd.
Glendale, CA
818-241-8099
www.borders.com

United States Adaptive Recreation Center - USARC
PO Box 2897
Big Bear Lake, CA 92315-2897
909-584-0269
USARC@bigbear.com
www.usarc.org

Telluride Adaptive Ski Program-TASP
PO Box 3354
Telluride, CO 81435
970-728-7537
tasp@telluridecoloradol.net
www.skitasp.org

Disabled Sports USA - Tahoe Adaptive Ski School
PO Box 9780
Truckee, CA 96162
530-581-4161
dsusatahoe@truckee.net
www.dsusafw.org

Northridge Hospital Medical Center
Driver Preparation Program
18300 Roscoe Blvd.
Northridge, CA 91328
818-885-5460

NORA – Neuro Optometric Rehabilitation Association
An organization for treatment of those with TBI that affects
their vision
www.nora.cc

Operation Discovery Program - Outreach
Reduced rates for nonprofit organizations
Mark Taper Forum and Ahmanson Theatre
Group Services
135 N. Grand Ave.
Los Angeles, CA 90012
213-972-7231
www.taperahmanson.com

Camp's Reading Refresher Program

Recording For the Blind and Dyslexic (RFB&D)
Learning through listening
20 Roszel Road
Princeton, NJ 08540
609-452-0606
www.rfbd.org
custserv@rfbd.org

Dr. Raymond H. M. Schaerf (Implanted Defibrillator)
Thoracic and Cardiovascular Surgery
2501 West Alameda Ave.
Burbank, CA 91505
818-843-2334

Hiring Tutors
Call the employment office at your local college

Medtronic (manufacturer of defibrillators)
7000 Central Ave. NE
Minneapolis, MN 55432-3576
612-574-4000 / 800-551-5544
www.medtronic.net

Sharper Image
Ultra 8 Wireless RF Electronic Locator S1676
Locator puts a pager on all elusive things
800-344-4444
www.sharperimage.com

TAIX Workout Studio
Linda Taix, Owner
Certified Fitness Trainer
1424 Foothill Blvd.
La Canada, CA 91011
818-790-7727

New Pathways-Center for Rehabilitation
Daniel Freeman Hospital
233 N. Prairie Ave.
Inglewood, CA 90301
310-674-7050 Ext. 3100

Department of Rehabilitation
Vocational Rehabilitation
425 W. Broadway, Suite 200
Glendale, CA 91204-1211
818-551-2147
www.dor.ca.gov

Convalescent Aid Society
Loan of Durable Medical Equipment
3255 E. Foothill Blvd.
626-793-1696

Donna McMillan
Organizing Offices and Homes
www.organizer4me.com
http://www.executiveletip.com